DAY OF THE DOG

I0139608

Daniel Damiano

BROADWAY PLAY PUBLISHING INC
New York
www.broadwayplaypublishing.com
info@broadwayplaypublishing.com

Cover photo by Carol Rosegg

First edition: February 2018
I S B N: 978-0-88145-757-5

Book design: Marie Donovan
Page make-up: Adobe InDesign
Typeface: Palatino

DAY OF THE DOG received its World Premiere with St. Louis Actors' Studio (William Roth, Producing Director; Milton Zoth, Artistic Director) at the Gaslight Theater in St. Louis in March/April 2013. The cast and creative contributors were:

PAUL .... Steve Isom
VADISLAV .... Jason Grubbe
JULIANNE .... Tamara Kenny

Director .... Milton Zoth
Production stage manager .... Amy J Paige
Set design .... Cristie Johnston
Costume design .... Teresa Doggett
Lighting design .... Jonathan Zelezniak
Sound design .... Milton Zoth
Props .... Carla Evans
Technical director .... G P Hunsaker

The production transferred to 59E59 Theatre in New York in March 2014. The cast and creative contributors were the same, with the exception of:

JULIANNE .... Michelle Hand

Special Thanks to the following organizations where DAY OF THE DOG received public readings prior to its World Premiere: Last Frontier Theatre Conference, Kitchen Dog Theatre New Works Festival, and the WorkShop Theater Company.

Also, thanks to the following actors for their performances in these readings; Judy Alvarez, Anne Caston, Frank Collison, Laura Gardner, Ken Glickfeld, Timothy Scott Harris, John Kaiser, Glenn Morshower and Harold Phillips.

CHARACTERS

PAUL, *early-to-mid 40s. Husband to* JULIANNE. *An accountant at a small firm. Ultimately, yields to Julianne regarding most issues. Contends with a diluted confidence, which he tries to overcome. Personable, more instinctive, countering* JULIANNE'*s practicality.*

VADISLAV, *early-to-mid 50s. A Canine Relations Specialist. He has, what appears to be, a Russian accent. It is this accent, coupled with his undying frankness, that may, initially, give the impression that he is stern. However, he can also be quite pleasant, humorous, charismatic and empathetic.*

JULIANNE, *early-to-mid 40s. Wife to* PAUL. *A successful, self-employed interior designer. She is vibrant, strong-willed, thorough, with a tendency to be guarded, which masks a suppressed vulnerability.*

SETTING

The play is set in the living area within the exquisitely designed home of JULIANNE *and* PAUL *(as well as daughter Brittany and dog Carrot) in South Florida.*

Summer.

The time is the present. A single day.

Suggested setting: A spacious, immaculately designed living room.

To make a blanket statement as to its décor, it should create an overall welcoming vibe while also maintaining a sense that it is for display more than to be lived in. There are predominately light colors and tones throughout (sea blue, teal, tan, etc.), a couple of simple, modern seascape paintings, bowls of beach stones and shells, a clay vase or two and some crystals. It should be evident that this is a professionally designed home with a fairly strong sense of designer Feng Shui. In keeping with this, there should be an absence of any overtly sharp objects or clutter of any kind.

The livingroom should contain a stylish couch with matching chairs, along with coffee table (atop which sit a bowl of beach stones and a medium size crystal). There can be strategically placed bookcases or tables, which may contain a select few family pictures, statuettes, etc.

*The main entrance door should be visible, as should the hallway entrances to the offstage kitchen/dining areas, guest bathroom/*JULIANNE's *office area and an entryway* *to the backyard/screen door area (where Carrot resides for the duration of play.) There can also be a visible stairway leading to the unseen second floor.*

For my wife, Judy Alvarez

ACT ONE

(Darkness)

(Doorbell)

(Lights up on PAUL, *who has several bandages about his forearms. He stands at the opened door.* VADISLAV *stands outside with a small handbag.)*

PAUL: *(With an eager smile...)* Hi. Vladimir?

VADISLAV: Vadislav.

PAUL: Right. Sorry. Thank you so much for coming.

VADISLAV: It's fine.

PAUL: Did you find us okay?

VADISLAV: Yes.

PAUL: Good. Did you hit much traffic?

VADISLAV: No.

PAUL: Oh, wonderful. It's a good time of day to travel, so you probably...

VADISLAV: Yes.

PAUL: Yes. Please, come in. I have you standing out there like...

VADISLAV: Thank you.

(...as VADISLAV *takes a few steps in:)*

PAUL: Oh, sure. Anyway, thank you so much for coming, again...

VADISLAV: It's fine.

PAUL: I know you're quite in demand…

VADISLAV: It's fine.

PAUL: We're lucky you could fit us in on such short notice…

VADISLAV: Yes.

PAUL: Yes, so…

VADISLAV: Where is the dog?

PAUL: Sure, I can show you to him. He's out back…

VADISLAV: No, not yet.

PAUL: Oh. Sorry.

VADISLAV: It's fine. The dog is Carol, you said?

PAUL: Carrot.

VADISLAV: Carrot?

PAUL: Yes.

VADISLAV: Like vegetable? Carrot?

PAUL: Yes, that's right.

VADISLAV: I wrote down "Carol".

PAUL: Oh, well,…no, it's Carrot.

VADISLAV: Carrot.

PAUL: Right.

VADISLAV: *(Jots in palm pilot…)* Your wife?

PAUL: Um…no, actually, he was already named at the shelter.

VADISLAV: I meant your wife's name.

PAUL: *(A nervous snicker…)* Oh. Sorry. Julianne.

VADISLAV: *(As he jots…)* Like potato?

PAUL: I'm sorry?

VADISLAV: Like Julianne Potato?

PAUL: *(A nervous snicker…)* Um…actually, no. That's Juli*enne*. She's Juli*anne*. With an A.

VADISLAV: Julianne with an A.

PAUL: Yes, J-U-L-I-A…

VADISLAV: You have offspring.

PAUL: Offspri…? Oh, yes. Our daughter.

VADISLAV: You only have the one.

PAUL: Yes.

VADISLAV: And her name?

PAUL: Brittany.

VADISLAV: Like Spears?

PAUL: *(A snicker…)* Um, no. More like the province.

VADISLAV: *(Jots…)* I see. So you liked the province.

PAUL: Yes, you can say that.

VADISLAV: So let's say that.

PAUL: *(A beat, a weak snicker…)* Well,…alright.

VADISLAV: You said Carrot is in the back?

PAUL: Yes, I can show you…

VADISLAV: No, not yet, please.

PAUL: Right, sorry.

VADISLAV: That's fine. I don't intend to approach Carrot until I've met with the family.

PAUL: Oh. Alright. *(A beat)* Well, my wife should be off the phone shortly. She's in the middle of a business call, but she's looking forward to meeting you.

VADISLAV: I see.

PAUL: Would you like to…?

VADISLAV: *(Steps in further, takes in house…)* Do only the two of you live here?

PAUL: Um, no, our daughter does too.

VADISLAV: Well, I'll need to speak with her as well.

PAUL: Oh, but…she's… She's not home now.

VADISLAV: Well, she'll need to be here.

PAUL: She's at band practice. She won't be back for a couple of hours.

VADISLAV: That will not work.

PAUL: I'm…I'm sorry, what won't work?

VADISLAV: I am here now.

PAUL: Yes. O…okay.

VADISLAV: Yes.

PAUL: *(Slight pause, an awkward grin…)* I'm sorry, I think I'm missing something. Do…?

VADISLAV: The problem lies in Carrot's relationship to everyone in this house. Therefore, the only way the relationship will stand a chance of improving is if all the parties involved are willing to participate. Otherwise, my purpose here is superfluous.

PAUL: Well, I'm sure it won't be *that*….

VADISLAV: Let me ask you something, does Carrot *growl* at Brittany?

PAUL: Well, yes, he's…

VADISLAV: Does he *bark* at Brittany?

PAUL: Yes, on occasion, he's…

VADISLAV: Does he *snap* at Brittany?

PAUL: Well, not yet, but…

VADISLAV: Alright, then how will Brittany's absence be beneficial?

PAUL: Well, I'm sorry, I just thought all you'd really need was...Carrot.

VADISLAV: Remedying Carrot's behavior is not the issue, nor is it my function.

PAUL: Oh. Well...

VADISLAV: I mentioned that when we set the appointment.

PAUL: *(A weak snicker...)* Well, I guess I misheard you...

VADISLAV: Regardless, it was mentioned.

PAUL: *(Slight pause)* O...okay...

VADISLAV: A dog is merely being a dog, just as all domestic animals are merely being animals. However, whether they've been trained to fetch or trained to kill stems from human interference. So my function here is to adjust the behavior of everyone who comes in contact with Carrot, thereby adjusting Carrot's behavior.

PAUL: Alri...yes, I understand. That's...yes. Well, we'll...it's important enough to us, so...

(JULIANNE enters briskly, smiling...)

JULIANNE: Hello. You must be the doggy doctor?

VADISLAV: No.

JULIANNE: No?

VADISLAV: You must be the wife.

JULIANNE: Yes. I'm Julianne.

VADISLAV: Julianne, yes!

JULIANNE: And you are?

PAUL: This is Vossilov, honey.

VADISLAV: Vadislav.

PAUL: Vadislav. I'm so sorry.

VADISLAV: That's fine.

PAUL: Vadislav.

JULIANNE: *(With a smile, to* VADISLAV*)* And you're…

PAUL: Vadislav.

JULIANNE: No, I've got the name, Paul. I'm asking his…

VADISLAV: I'm a Canine Relations Specialist.

JULIANNE: Oh. So you *are* who we were expecting.

VADISLAV: Yes, I suppose I am then.

JULIANNE: *(Half joking)* I'm sorry, the others considered themselves dog *therapists*, dog *probers*…

VADISLAV: I see.

JULIANNE: I can't keep up with the terminologies you all have.

VADISLAV: I only have one.

PAUL: I sort of lost track myself.

VADISLAV: Well, now we know.

PAUL: Oh, yes. Absolutely.

(…as PAUL *snickers, filling the air…)*

JULIANNE: *(Through an urgent smile…)* Honey, did he meet Carrot?

PAUL: He…

VADISLAV: No.

PAUL: He wants to meet with us first.

VADISLAV: Yes.

JULIANNE: *(Oddly, then with a smile…)* Oh. Well, alright. That's fine. How long do you think this will take?

VADISLAV: I can't give you a time frame.

JULIANNE: Well, can you try? I have some business that I'll need to tend to, so…

VADISLAV: Again, I can't give you a time frame. We are done when we are done.

JULIANNE: I'm sorry?

PAUL: He'd like to have Brittany here too.

VADISLAV: Yes.

JULIANNE: *(With a feigned grin, to* PAUL*)* Why?

VADISLAV: I'm here. You can ask me.

JULIANNE: *(A beat)* Alright. Why?

VADISLAV: Because Brittany is a part of this family, yes.

JULIANNE: *(A beat)* Well, yes, but she's leaving for Europe tomorrow.

VADISLAV: I thought she was at band practice.

JULIANNE: She *is* at band practice.

VADISLAV: But not in Europe.

JULIANNE: No, she's at school, and she's there because *tomorrow* she'll be going with her school band to a prestigious musical competition in Austria.

VADISLAV: So *today* she is at school.

JULIANNE: Yes.

VADISLAV: So she is not far from home, yes?

JULIANNE: *(A beat, a strained grin)* Paul, I'm not getting this.

PAUL: Honey...

VADISLAV: What is there to get?

PAUL: Julianne, he's...

JULIANNE: *(To* VADISLAV, *attempting politeness)* Well, frankly, we didn't have to go through this with the others.

PAUL: *(Apologetically, to* VADISLAV...*)* No, that's true but...

VADISLAV: Were the others able to resolve this issue?

JULIANNE: Excuse me?

VADISLAV: Has the situation with Carrot been remedied or am I here for a reason?

PAUL: Well, no, you're…

JULIANNE: (Over "…you're…") Paul, wait a second. Voslov, can you…?

VADISLAV: Vadislav.

JULIANNE: I'm sorry. *Vadislav,* would you mind if my husband and I …?

VADISLAV: That's fine. May I use your bathroom?

JULIANNE: Um…

PAUL: Sure, it's through the kitchen, to your left.

(VADISLAV *nods, and goes off.*)

JULIANNE: I thought you were handling this, Paul.

PAUL: What do you mean? I am handling this…

JULIANNE: He doesn't know us from Adam, and yet he wants to renovate my schedule, Brittany's schedule…

PAUL: I didn't know he'd require all this

JULIANNE: How could you not know, Paul? He didn't mention this to you prior?

PAUL: Well, he might've but I mean, hey, we're lucky enough to get him on such short notice.

JULIANNE: Lucky?

PAUL: He's booked like five months ahead. He travels all over the country. I told you I happened to call just as he had a cancellation. He didn't have to do that.

JULIANNE: I don't think he was doing us any favors, Paul.

PAUL: Julianne, he's supposed to be very good.

JULIANNE: Well, of course he's *supposed* to be. Anybody that considers them self a professional is, by definition, *supposed* to be very good at what they do. It doesn't mean they are.

PAUL: Well,...y'know, let's just give him a chance, okay...?

JULIANNE: We'll give him a chance, but I cannot take up my day with this.

PAUL: You won't have to...

JULIANNE: And he wants us to pull Brittany away from band practice? Are you kidding me?

PAUL: It'll be fine. This is not gonna' adversely affect her...

JULIANNE: Paul, I am not pulling Brittany out of band practice. What do you mean *it'll be fine*?

PAUL: Julianne...

JULIANNE: How much is this, anyway?

PAUL: I don't know.

JULIANNE: You don't know?!

PAUL: He wouldn't give me a number.

JULIANNE: I don't understand. Paul, you need to ask.

PAUL: I *did* ask. He...

JULIANNE: What do you mean he wouldn't give you a number?

PAUL: He just said he'd bring it up when the time is right.

JULIANNE: What?

PAUL: Julianne...

JULIANNE: So, what, he's gonna' have us all gather around Carrot like some intervention, wave a wand

over his head, do nothing, and then nail us for five
thousand dollars?

PAUL: No, he won't

JULIANNE: Oh, no? How much money've we thrown
away on the other gurus, Paul?

PAUL: If this…

JULIANNE: We may as well've booked Deepak Chopra,
for Godsakes.

PAUL: If this works, it'll be worth it, okay? And I think
this…

(VADISLAV *appears out of nowhere, behind* JULIANNE…)

VADISLAV: Do…?

JULIANNE: AHHHH!

VADISLAV: I'm sorry. Did I scare you?

JULIANNE: *(Regathering somewhat…)* No, of course not. I
just didn't see you come back in.

VADISLAV: I see. Do you have soap?

JULIANNE: Soap?

VADISLAV: There was no soap in the bathroom.

JULIANNE: Yes, there is. It's in the bowl next to the
faucet.

VADISLAV: I saw a bowl but nothing that resembled
soap.

JULIANNE: Yes, there's most certainly soap. There's a
rosemary soap bar in the bowl.

VADISLAV: That's soap?

JULIANNE: Yes, it's soap.

VADISLAV: Very unusual.

JULIANNE: Yes, well, still and all,…it's soap. Excuse me,
how much are your services, sir?

VADISLAV: *(With a smile)* We'll discuss that when the time is right.

PAUL: Julianne...

JULIANNE: *(With an equal smile...)* Well, the time is perfectly fine for me now, if you don't mind. I'd really like to know.

VADISLAV: I cannot make a financial assessment when I've yet to assess the situation.

JULIANNE: What's to assess? We have a dog who has behavioral issues. How much do you charge to remedy this situation?

VADISLAV: That is not how this works.

PAUL: Julianne...

JULIANNE: Well, how **does** this work?

VADISLAV: May I please wash my hands before we continue this discussion?

JULIANNE: I really...

PAUL: *(Over "...really...")* Yes, that's fine.

VADISLAV: Thank you. *(He goes off...)*

PAUL: Look, everything will be fine. This shouldn't take too much of your time.

JULIANNE: Paul, how did you even find him?

PAUL: I told you. He was recommended by Jim.

JULIANNE: Who's Jim?

PAUL: You know Jim, right?

JULIANNE: Obviously, I don't.

PAUL: He works with me at the firm. Didn't I introduce you to him at Sam's barbecue?

JULIANNE: Who?

PAUL: Sam.

JULIANNE: Who is *he*?!

PAUL: We were at his house in Boca a couple of summers ago.

JULIANNE: I don't know him, Paul…

PAUL: He made that amazing brisket.

JULIANNE: I don't remember him, Paul…

PAUL: His wife is…

JULIANNE: *Regardless*, you feel that Jim is a reliable source?

PAUL: Yes. And I'm sure his cousin is too.

JULIANNE: What do you mean his "cousin" is?

PAUL: He has a cousin in Baltimore. He hired him and told Jim about it, and Jim told me.

JULIANNE: So, wait, this isn't even a first-hand recommendation?

PAUL: Well, Jim doesn't have a dog, Julianne, so…

JULIANNE: Paul, my God, we should at least have a reputable referral.

PAUL: Jim's cousin is totally reputable. I mean, *Jim* is. I work with him.

JULIANNE: And he makes great brisket, right?

PAUL: No, that's Sam.

JULIANNE: Whoever, Paul. I don't like this…

PAUL: Look, however he works, I think it'll be worth it.

JULIANNE: You do.

PAUL: Yes, okay? This guy's method is a little more interactive, which I think is the way to go here. That's probably why nothing's worked with Carrot. Maybe he just needs everyone around in order for something to take effect.

JULIANNE: And you're willing to pull Brittany out of practice for one of the biggest experiences of her life for this.

PAUL: Yes, I...

JULIANNE: Paul, I can't believe this...

PAUL: Look, don't you think this whole situation with Carrot has had some adverse effect on Brittany?

JULIANNE: What are you talking about?

PAUL: You haven't noticed how she's been colder? Sarcastic? She doesn't make small talk anymore.

JULIANNE: Small talk? Paul, we're her parents, not a blind date.

PAUL: I'm saying that her personality has changed.

JULIANNE: Whatever has changed in her is not because of...

(VADISLAV *again appears behind* JULIANNE...)

VADISLAV: Dogs...

JULIANNE: AHHH!

VADISLAV: I apologize.

JULIANNE: *(Holding heart...)* Jesus Christ.

VADISLAV: I was just going to say that dogs respond to contempt.

JULIANNE: *Contempt?*

VADISLAV: Dogs are very sensitive. They can sense many things.

JULIANNE: I can assure you no one has contempt for Carrot. He's much loved.

VADISLAV: Perhaps Carrot feels differently.

JULIANNE: What does *that* mean?

PAUL: Julianne...

VADISLAV: I'm right here. I'll be happy to speak for myself.

PAUL: Oh. Well,… Okay.

VADISLAV: Do you do this often?

PAUL: Do…what often?

VADISLAV: Speak for someone else in front of that very someone.

PAUL: Oh, well…I'm sorry.

VADISLAV: No apologies, please. I'm asking because I'm curious if this is a common way for the family to relate to each other.

JULIANNE: Look, I very much appreciate your intent here, but you can be anybody off the street who's walked into our home posing as whatever you say you are…

PAUL: Julianne…

VADISLAV: That's true, but I'm not.

JULIANNE: Alright. Honey, have you asked for proof of who he is or if he's licensed?

PAUL: Um, well…

VADISLAV: I will be happy to show you everything.

(The phone rings…)

JULIANNE: I have to get that. Paul, will you please?

PAUL: What?

JULIANNE: *(In a firm but slightly hushed tone, smiling.)* Handle this situation, please. Thank you! *(She rushes off…)*

(A beat. PAUL is somewhat embarrassed.)

(VADISLAV picks up on this.)

VADISLAV: Perhaps we should cancel.

PAUL: No, please, that's... This...she'll be fine. She's... Her career is really burgeoning at the moment so, y'know, maybe the timing isn't the best but...we'll... It'll be fine.

VADISLAV: Do you believe this?

PAUL: I...ye...I, yes, I do. I mean, you probably get this to some degree anyway, right?

VADISLAV: Get what?

PAUL: Well,...skepticism.

VADISLAV: I can tell you that I am often hired after previous efforts with other so-called professionals have failed. So there may be an initial trepidation, but there is ultimately a mutual willingness to do what is necessary.

(PAUL absorbs this, nods, looks off sheepishly in JULIANNE'S *direction...)*

PAUL: *(A beat)* How soon would we be able to reschedule you?

VADISLAV: December, at the earliest.

PAUL: No, no, she'll...we'll... I mean, we have to do this. There's...there's no choice in the matter.

VADISLAV: There is a choice. You can seek somebody whose methods are more preferable. I think that may be wise.

PAUL: I'd really...I'd really prefer to resolve this as soon as possible.

VADISLAV: I'm sure there are others who can help.

PAUL: Well, we've tried others and, well, here we are so...I'd... This will work. I'm certain. She'll...I mean, my God, it **has** to or else we'll just have to...

VADISLAV: *(A beat)* Have to what?

PAUL: *(Then, sheepishly...)* Well, I...I wasn't gonna' say put him down or anything.

VADISLAV: I should hope not.

PAUL: *(A forced snicker...)* No, not at all. Not..., no, no, not at...not at all. I just... *(A beat, as he looks in* JULIANNE's *direction.)* Look, as soon as she gets off the phone, I'll call our daughter, okay? Brittany has her cell and her own car. She can be here in a half hour, alright? Julianne'll...she'll be fine with this. She... she's just... You know, her head's somewhere else, but we'll...she'll...

VADISLAV: You're sure.

PAUL: Yes, abso...absolutely.

VADISLAV: Very well.

PAUL: Alright?

VADISLAV: That's fine.

PAUL: I'm so sorry about this.

VADISLAV: It's fine.

PAUL: Is there anything you need?

VADISLAV: Need?

PAUL: Would you like something? Some water, soda...?

VADISLAV: Tunafish will be fine.

PAUL: Tuna...tunafish?

VADISLAV: Yes, please.

PAUL: Is...is that something that you like to work with?

VADISLAV: No, it's something that I like to eat.

PAUL: Oh. O...okay.

VADISLAV: Solid white in Albacore on pumpernickel, if you have it.

PAUL: Well, I'll...I'll see.

VADISLAV: Thank you.

PAUL: And to drink?

VADISLAV: Vodka, if you have.

PAUL: Vodka?

VADISLAV: Two fingers, no more, please.

PAUL: Oh. Well, okay. I'll…yeah, I think we…have it.
(A beat, a snicker) I guess it makes sense, right?

VADISLAV: What makes sense?

PAUL: Well, you're from Russia, right?

VADISLAV: No.

PAUL: *(A beat…)* No?

VADISLAV: No.

PAUL: Well,…then…just outside of Russia then.

VADISLAV: No.

PAUL: Eastern Europe?

VADISLAV: No.

(An odd moment, as PAUL *can no longer grasp at geographical straws…)*

PAUL: Okay, well…I'll be right back. Okay?

*(*VADISLAV *nods, as* PAUL *exits.* VADISLAV *sits on couch. He takes in the room, until his cell phone blares to the song "Who Let the Dogs Out". He swiftly retrieves phone from his waste holster, followed by his palm pilot…)*

VADISLAV: Yes? —Yes, this is he. —How old is the dog? —Name? —Of the dog? —Lute? —Lute, like instrument? —Luke! Like the *Cool Hand* Luke, yes. — You are the owner? —Your name? —Address? —Any other animals? —I have an opening on December 3rd. —Yes, I am aware that it is five months away. December 3rd? —Very well, I will call you on December 2nd for directions. —We will discuss that when I have made an assessment. And please make certain that everyone who resides in your home is present for our appointment. —Yes, *everyone*. —Good day. *(He clicks off...)*

JULIANNE: *(Offstage)* PAUL...?! *(She enters urgently...)*

VADISLAV: *(Smiling pleasantly)* He is in the kitchen.

JULIANNE: The kitchen?

VADISLAV: Yes.

JULIANNE: I heard music.

VADISLAV: That was my cell phone. I apologize.

JULIANNE: What's going on?

VADISLAV: Nothing is going on. We're waiting for you.

JULIANNE: Waiting for...? Excuse me. PAUL...?!!!

(JULIANNE goes to kitchen entryway, where PAUL comes out with an elegantly prepared sandwich and a glass of vodka.)

PAUL: I'm right here. You're off the phone?

JULIANNE: *(In a slightly hushed tone...)* What is this? You're having *lunch* now?

PAUL: *(The same tone)* It's for him.

JULIANNE: Are you kidding me?

PAUL: I asked if he needed anything and this is what he needed.

JULIANNE: A sandwich?

PAUL: He has to wait so it's only proper that we offer him a nice meal, Julianne.

JULIANNE: Paul, I'm tenuous enough about him being here, let alone him having lunch here.

PAUL: Julianne...

JULIANNE: I asked you to handle this.

PAUL: I am. Just because I made him a tuna fish sandwich and vodka doesn't mean that I'm not...

JULIANNE: That's vodka?!

PAUL: Yes, alright?

JULIANNE: Paul, are you aware that this afternoon I am to have a very important teleconference call with two West Coast T V producers?

PAUL: Yes, I know...

JULIANNE: I don't think you do, Paul, because this is a distraction.

PAUL: How is this a distraction?

JULIANNE: You think I can focus when I have a strange man drinking vodka in my living room?

PAUL: Julianne, your meeting is not for a couple of hours, right? He might not even be here by then.

JULIANNE: But he's here *now* and you're serving him alcohol.

PAUL: He's not from here, Julianne. I'm sure he has a higher threshold for alcohol, alright?

JULIANNE: Are you trying to be funny?

PAUL: No, I'm... There's nothing to worry about, okay?

JULIANNE: Paul...

PAUL: Just trust me here. I...can you just do that? You left it to me to handle this, I'm handling it. He's not a threat. He's licensed and board certified.

JULIANNE: You know this.

PAUL: I'm...sure he is.

JULIANNE: Did he show you proof?

PAUL: I didn't ask. You did.

JULIANNE: Paul, you *have* to ask these questions...

PAUL: If you want to see proof, he'll show it to you. You left the room before he could, alright? I believe him. I mean, geez, what does it matter if he's certified anyway? The others were and they couldn't do anything, right?

JULIANNE: Yeah, and whose fault is that?

PAUL: I'm aware that... Look, he's already remedied the behavior of a Rott Weiler who happens to be the pet of a cousin of a co-worker of mine, okay?

JULIANNE: Yes, of course. "Sam".

PAUL: No, Jim.

JULIANNE: Fine. Jim.

PAUL: Yeah, so...y'know? I mean, that's proof enough that this guy is the real deal, right?

JULIANNE: You don't know that, Paul.

PAUL: I have a good feeling about this, okay? Now do you have a few minutes so we can just speak with him together?

JULIANNE: (A beat) Brittany is not coming out of band practice for this.

PAUL: Julianne...

JULIANNE: Absolutely not, Paul. If he's a professional, he should be able to work under whatever circumstances are provided, just as I do. Now I will give him the limited time that I am willing and able to give. Beyond that, if I find him to be respectable, he will deal with you. If that's not enough, he can take his tuna sandwich to go, but the plate stays.

PAUL: Alright, but...

JULIANNE: And I'm letting in Carrot soon. It's too humid for him to be out this long.

PAUL: But he said...

(The phone rings, JULIANNE *starts off…)*

JULIANNE: *(With a sudden bright smile…)* We're not arguing about this, Paul. Now that's Brian. I have to give him my fabric orders.

PAUL: Well, can you call him back at least?

JULIANNE: This is my business. I have deadlines…

PAUL: Yes, I know but…

JULIANNE: I'll be there when I'm there. Just tell this guy to keep his pants on. *Literally. (She exits.)*

*(*PAUL *remains, somewhat distressed, before coming into the living room…)*

PAUL: *(A broad but forced smile….)* Here you go, Voslov. *(…presents plate, napkin, coaster & glass on coffee table.)*

VADISLAV: Vadislav.

PAUL: Sorry. Vadislav. Let me say that a few times to get it into my head; Vadislav, Vadislav, Vadislav, Vadislav, *Vadislav.* Alright there we go.

VADISLAV: Very good.

PAUL: Anything else while you're waiting?

VADISLAV: No, this will be plenty. Thank you.

PAUL: You're quite welcome. I'm just glad we had everything.

VADISLAV: Yes. It looks wonderful.

PAUL: Julianne just has to take this one call and then she'll be out with us. It shouldn't take too long.

VADISLAV: Very nice preparation.

PAUL: I'm sorry?

VADISLAV: The sandwich.

PAUL: Oh. Well,…thank you.

VADISLAV: You were either a chef in a past life or in the current one.

PAUL: *(A weakly prideful grin)* Wow. Actually,...I did graduate from culinary school.

VADISLAV: So you *are* a chef.

PAUL: Oh, no...I'm, no. I'm an accountant.

VADISLAV: An accountant.

PAUL: Yes, mhm.

VADISLAV: Why is that?

PAUL: *(A beat, an awkward snicker)* Why...why am I an accountant? Um...well, I already had my accounting degree.

VADISLAV: But then you went to culinary school.

PAUL: Yes, that's...

VADISLAV: Because you did not want to be an accountant?

PAUL: I...well, *at the time*, yes, that's true. I mean, my father had his own firm, so...it was sort of expected of me.

VADISLAV: *He* expected it of you.

PAUL: Uh...yes, you can...

VADISLAV: But you wanted to be a chef.

PAUL: Yes, I...at the time, yes.

VADISLAV: I see.

PAUL: I did cook briefly, but then...things weren't working out as planned, so...

VADISLAV: So...you decided to pursue accounting.

PAUL: Yes, that's...yes.

VADISLAV: Why did things not work out?

PAUL: *(A beat)* Um...well, it's...I just...as I said, it didn't work out as I'd anticipated.

VADISLAV: Yes, you said that much.

PAUL: Yes.

(A moment, as VADISLAV *continues to wait for* PAUL *to elaborate.)*

PAUL: *(Brightly, at first...)* Well, I just...I was a Sous chef at this French restaurant, straight out of culinary school, which was...you know, very exciting,...until they fired me. So...that's it.

VADISLAV: Well, that certainly doesn't seem very fair.

PAUL: Yes. Well, it...wasn't that cut'n dried, actually.

*(*VADISLAV, *again, awaits* PAUL's *elaboration for a moment before* PAUL *reluctantly...)*

PAUL: I undercooked a Chicken Cordon Bleu. At least that was the...conclusion.

VADISLAV: Well, that happens.

PAUL: *(A beat, with a strained smile...)* And it...made a patron sick and...he vomited all over the table...and several other tables...and patrons. And the patron that got sick...happened to be a prominent critic from the *Times*. And so he ended up documenting the...events... in a...fairly...scathing review, which eventually... closed the place down.

VADISLAV: *(Slight pause, a grin)* So you decided to pursue accounting.

PAUL: Yes, that's...eventually, yes. *(With a forced smile, a false bravado.)* But, hey, I've managed to...you know, do pretty well for myself.

VADISLAV: Yes?

PAUL: Oh,…yes. I'm at a small, local firm,…but I find that there's a better sense of appreciation than at the larger firms.

VADISLAV: You've worked at the larger firms?

PAUL: Well, um…no, but…that's…my assumption.

VADISLAV: Well, your wife also works, yes?

PAUL: *(A beat)* Yes, that's…yes.

VADISLAV: She is successful, yes?

PAUL: She's…yes, very much so, yes…

VADISLAV: So there's not pressure on you to solely provide.

PAUL: Yes,…that's right. Well, I mean, it's…quite common, right?

VADISLAV: What is common?

PAUL: Well, you know,…dual incomes in a marriage.

VADISLAV: Is it?

PAUL: *(Slight pause)* I…yeah, it…yes, it is. I mean, *here* it is.

VADISLAV: In the house?

PAUL: No, I mean,…the country.

VADISLAV: Does that make it easier or more difficult for you?

PAUL: *(An awkward snicker…)* I…well, I…no, it… Wow, that's a pointed question, isn't it?

VADISLAV: Is it?

PAUL: Well,…no, not…not really. We've…I think we've maintained a…fairly decent balance,…more or less, I mean, granted, when I went through a less desirable period, after the…

VADISLAV: Chicken Cordon Bleu.

PAUL: Ye…yes. After that, Julianne sort of picked up the slack for us, certainly. But then, when she became pregnant with our daughter, and we decided to move, I sort of did the same, while she raised Brittany and started to make her connections down here. And, of course, that led to…

VADISLAV: Yes.

PAUL: Yes. Of course I've always supported Julianne in her pursuits and…now, God, she's gonna' even have her own show and I couldn't be prouder of her.

VADISLAV: A show.

PAUL: Oh, yes.

VADISLAV: She's an actress?

PAUL: No, she's an Interior Designer/Philosopher.

VADISLAV: *Designer/Philosopher?*

PAUL: Yes. She has degrees in both and married them into one profession, basically.

VADISLAV: Interesting.

PAUL: Yeah, it really is. And now there's a lot of home repair, home design, home makeover shows so she's sort of riding that wave.

VADISLAV: I see.

PAUL: But she's by no means a fly-by-night, y'know? I mean, she's worked very hard.

VADISLAV: I'm sure.

PAUL: You can see it in our house.

VADISLAV: Yes.

PAUL: She's fairly meticulous.

VADISLAV: Yes.

PAUL: Color schemes. Space allocation.

VADISLAV: Yes, yes. I also love the various accoutrements.

(...*as* VADISLAV *casually picks up a large Amethyst crystal from the coffee table and admires it, observed somewhat nervously by* PAUL...)

PAUL: Yes. That's...what is that? I think it's a...

VADISLAV: Amethyst Crystal.

PAUL: Yes, that's... I think you're right.

(VADISLAV *places crystal back down, perhaps an inch to the left of where it was prior...*)

PAUL: Um...let me just...move that back a bit. (*He moves crystal back to its original place, then resumes with a sudden smile...*) Yeah, she even designed Carrot's doghouse.

VADISLAV: Really?

PAUL: (*A weak snicker*) Oh, yes. Carpeting, a sun roof, Buddhist fountain, happy colors. I think his is the only dog house that can be declared good Feng Shui.

VADISLAV: Feng Shui.

PAUL: Yes. Do you know what that is?

VADISLAV: Of course. Feng Shui stems from Chinese tradition. It focuses on one creating a living environment which is harmonious with the earth.

PAUL: Very good. Yes.

VADISLAV: Thank you.

(VADISLAV *takes another bite, as* PAUL...)

PAUL: (*With a grin of forced assurance...*) Um... Vadislav, my wife feels that it isn't necessary that Brittany...

(*A loud bark and intense scratching from the offstage sliding door jolts* PAUL...)

PAUL: AH!

(The sounds do not remotely phase VADISLAV, *who enjoys his sandwich…)*

VADISLAV: You were saying?

PAUL: Yes, sorry. Julianne feels that…that…

(The barks and scratches continue, while noticeably unsettling PAUL…)

JULIANNE: *(Offstage…)* PAUL, WILL YOU LET CARROT IN, PLEASE?!

PAUL: *(Slight pause)* Um…what…what was that, honey?

JULIANNE: WHAT?!

PAUL: I…I couldn't…I COULDN'T HEAR YOU TOO WELL!

JULIANNE: WILL YOU LET CARROT IN?! HE WANTS TO COME IN!

VADISLAV: *(Without looking at* PAUL, *as he eats…)* Don't let Carrot in.

PAUL: Yes, that's…I agr…JULIANNE, VASLAV…

VADISLAV: Vadislav.

PAUL: Sorry…VADISLAV SUGGESTED THAT CARROT STAY OUT FOR NOW!

JULIANNE: PAUL, CARROT WANTS TO COME IN. CAN YOU HEAR HIM?!

VADISLAV: He needs to be outside for now.

PAUL: Yes,…JULIANNE, WE SHOULD MEET WITH VADISLAV FIRST BEFORE CARROT COMES IN. IT'S PART OF HIS…HIS METHOD.

JULIANNE: PAUL, I'M ON A BUSINESS CALL! CAN YOU LET HIM IN, PLEASE?! IT'S TOO HOT FOR HIM!!!

*(*VADISLAV *stops eating. Casually walks off in the direction of sliding door to the backyard, unbeknownst to* PAUL…)

PAUL: WELL, HONEY, HE HAS HIS LITTLE FOUNTAIN OUT THERE…!

JULIANNE: PAUL, HE WANTS TO COME IN! PUT HIS LEASH ON!

PAUL: WELL, THAT'S NOT VERY EASY TO…!!! I THINK HE JUST HEARS THE MAILMAN! YOU KNOW HOW EXCITED HE GETS WHEN…

JULIANNE: WHAT?!

PAUL: I SAID I THINK HE JUST HEARS THE MAIL…!!!

(PAUL *suddenly notices that the barking has stopped, before* VADISLAV *enters, casually, and resumes with sandwich.*)

PAUL: YOU SEE, HONEY! IT'S ALL GOOD! HE STOPPED! HE'S FINE! (*To* VADISLAV) Did *you* do that?

VADISLAV: Yes.

PAUL: My God, I didn't even hear the door.

VADISLAV: I didn't open it.

PAUL: Geez, usually the only thing that can stop him from going on like that is a muzzle, which I can barely put on him half the time….

VADISLAV: There is a symptom of your problem.

PAUL: What, the muzzle?

VADISLAV: That's an extension of your distrust. If you distrust him, then he won't trust you.

PAUL: Well, with all due respect to your profession, Vadislav…

VADISLAV: Humans have intellect, a brain of greater dimension, longer arms, legs… Many ways of conveying and displaying emotion. Dogs have two primary methods of such; the teeth and the tongue. What they display to you is only in return for what you display to them.

PAUL: Well, that's… I'll certainly give that thought.

VADISLAV: You have no choice. You have to make it a practice or else you have a situation that you have now. Maybe next time you go to the hospital, you come out with your arm amputated. This is a wonderful sandwich, by the way.

PAUL: *(Distracted by the word "amputated"…)* Oh, well… is…that's… I'm…glad you like it…

VADISLAV: Very well prepared. What kind of mayonnaise did you use, if you don't mind me asking?

PAUL: No, um…it's actually homemade, with Egg whites, Virgin Olive oil…um, a touch of curry and I…I put in a splash of lemon.

VADISLAV: Yes, that's it! Yes, the citrus gives it a very nice balance.

PAUL: Oh, well,…glad you like it.

VADISLAV: Very nice.

PAUL: Thank you.

(…as JULIANNE *comes out, with apparent concern…)*

(For a brief moment, she observes VADISLAV *eating and* PAUL *looking on, almost proudly…)*

JULIANNE: What's happening, Paul?

PAUL: Nothing. Are you…?

JULIANNE: Where's Carrot?

PAUL: He's fine. He's outside. Are you ready?

JULIANNE: What happened?

(…as JULIANNE *goes off towards the sliding door…)*

PAUL: *(With exaggerated enthusiasm)* Everything's fine. Vadislav just got him to stop barking. Isn't that something?!

VADISLAV: *(With a mouthful)* A simple hand gesture.

(...as JULIANNE *returns...)*

JULIANNE: What?

PAUL: He did some kinda' hand gesture. He didn't even open the door. Amazing, huh?

VADISLAV: *(With a mouthful...)* Very, very good.

JULIANNE: Excuse me?

VADISLAV: This is probably the best tuna sandwich I've ever had.

PAUL: Well, thank you, Vadislav.

VADISLAV: Excellent. There is fresh dill as well, yes?

PAUL: Yes, yes, there is...

JULIANNE: *(A sharp smile)* Can we start, please?

PAUL: Okay. I think we're ready, if you'd like to speak with both of us.

VADISLAV: I trust that Brittany is on her way?

PAUL: Um, well...

JULIANNE: *(Glancing at* PAUL...*)* No, actually I've already told Paul that I'd prefer not to pull her out of band practice for this, so...

PAUL: Julianne...

VADISLAV: This situation affects your daughter as much as the two of you.

JULIANNE: *(With a feigned smile)* Well, we are her parents so I'm sure anything you tell us, we can pass on to her.

VADISLAV: That is not how this works.

JULIANNE: *(A beat)* Well, I'm afraid that's how this will *have* to work, okay? Now if you'd like to speak to us, we're here, so...

VADISLAV: Let me ask you, do you feel Carrot likes Brittany given the behavior he exhibits toward her?

JULIANNE: Of course, he likes her.

VADISLAV: Really.

JULIANNE: Yes, he does.

VADISLAV: Have you witnessed Brittany with Carrot often?

JULIANNE: Often enough. A lot of the time, she's practicing in her room, so...

VADISLAV: With the door shut?

JULIANNE: Yes, but...

VADISLAV: So you have not seen them together that often, yes?

JULIANNE: I've seen them together enough to know that he likes her, but he can get aggressive at times.

VADISLAV: Aggressive in that he growls at her?

JULIANNE: There've been a few times, yes. But that's been the extent of it.

VADISLAV: Well, that is the extent to which I'm here. This is a concern of yours, yes?

JULIANNE: He loves Brittany. There are simply eccentricities of his behavior that we hope to rectify here, if you'd help us.

VADISLAV: And in order to do that, it would be of substantial benefit for her to be with us.

JULIANNE: *(To* PAUL*)* I can't believe this.

VADISLAV: If this were merely an eccentricity on *my* behalf, that is one thing. But this is something else. Because as it stands now, Brittany is one of the objects of Carrot's hostility. This is an issue of her safety. You care about that, yes?

JULIANNE: She's our daughter. How the hell can you ask a question like that?

VADISLAV: It is rhetorical. I'm sure you care for her well-being very much.

(JULIANNE *takes a moment, looks at* PAUL *then back at* VADISLAV...)

JULIANNE: May I see your license, please?

PAUL: Julianne...

VADISLAV: That is fine. You have every right to ask. (*Removes his license from his bag...*) Here you are. That is my Practitioner's License. I would advise you not to try and pronounce my last name. You'd have to sneeze once and cough twice to even come close.

(VADISLAV *laughs*, PAUL *accompanies...as* JULIANNE *analyzes his license...*)

VADISLAV: I also have this.

JULIANNE: What is it?

VADISLAV: This is a laminated letter of recommendation from the President of the Canine Coalition for Canine Development.

JULIANNE: I've never heard of them.

PAUL: Well, I'm sure it's a real organization, honey.

JULIANNE: I'm not saying it isn't. I'm just saying that I've never heard of them.

PAUL: Not everyone's heard of everything.

JULIANNE: Paul...

VADISLAV: There is a website address if you wish to investigate further.

PAUL: That won't be necessary, right, honey?

JULIANNE: Honey, am I even in the room or what?!

PAUL: Of course, you are. I'm just...

JULIANNE: This is our right as consumers. If I want to check and see if he is licensed or go to this website and verify if this organization is for real, that is totally my prerogative, alright?

VADISLAV: Absolutely.

PAUL: Alright, fine. I'm just saying, you're pressed for time and...

(JULIANNE *looks at* PAUL, *before returning the materials to* VADISLAV. *She then takes a contemplative moment, before begrudgingly...*)

JULIANNE: Alright, call her up. This is... She's in the middle of practice. She probably won't even have the ringer on.

PAUL: *(With sudden enthusiasm...)* She usually keeps it on vibrate, honey. You know that.

JULIANNE: Well, she shouldn't pick up. She should be focusing on her instrument.

PAUL: She'll be fine, okay? She may even have time to go back, n'if not, she can practice on her own tonight. It'll be fine. I'll be right back.

(PAUL *urgently goes off, while* VADISLAV *resumes with sandwich, alternating with an occasional sip of vodka.* JULIANNE *observes this, barely indulging...*)

VADISLAV: Mm, very good.

JULIANNE: Would you like a cigarette?

VADISLAV: I am fine, thank you. He is very talented, your husband. I take it that he makes most of the meals.

JULIANNE: Yes, he does.

VADISLAV: You are very fortunate.

JULIANNE: Look, Voltov...

VADISLAV: Vadislav.

JULIANNE: Fine, sorry. *Vadislav,* we've obviously made considerable accommodations in order to help you alleviate our problem with Carrot, but I'd really prefer it if you didn't come into my house and within a half hour tell me that I should be fortunate on the basis of a tuna sandwich. Alright?

VADISLAV: *(Genuinely)* I apologize. I didn't mean to suggest...

JULIANNE: Are you done with that plate? *(As she impatiently approaches table...)*

VADISLAV: This is not to say that Paul and Brittany are not fortunate to have you.

JULIANNE: *(Offguarded, before impatiently...)* Please, that's not what I'm...

VADISLAV: Because they are most fortunate, believe me. You've done a remarkable job designing this house. You did this, yes?

JULIANNE: Yes, I did.

VADISLAV: Not that my opinion means anything with regards to home design, but I have to say you have created a most captivating abode. It's absolutely beautiful.

JULIANNE: *(Slight pause, nearly flattered)* Well,...thank you. That's very kind.

VADISLAV: Please, it's honesty. I would imagine that there is little margin for kindness in your profession, yes?

JULIANNE: *(A beat, before a half grin...)* That's true.

VADISLAV: People are paying you to get what they want, yes?

JULIANNE: Oh, yes, that's...

VADISLAV: Or what they don't even know they want.

JULIANNE: Yes, exactly...

VADISLAV: Yes, I'm sure. Your husband tells me you are even about to have your own television show.

JULIANNE: *(A beat)* Well, I'm in negotiations...

VADISLAV: So that means it will happen.

JULIANNE: Well, it's not in stone, but...

VADISLAV: *(With pleasant but firm assurance)* It will happen. I am certain of it.

JULIANNE: *(A beat, a grin...)* Well,...I feel pretty strongly about it, I'll say that.

VADISLAV: As well you should.

JULIANNE: *(A beat, then with a certain pride...)* For now, they're...interested in the *idea* of me hosting a design show, but I requested to have creative input regarding format and concept, which I'm presenting today and, upon their approval, I could have something finalized.

VADISLAV: How exciting.

JULIANNE: Hm.

VADISLAV: And I take it you had desired this for some time?

JULIANNE: Well., it was certainly an aspiration.

VADISLAV: My, such a talented family.

JULIANNE: Well...

VADISLAV: And your daughter plays what instrument?

JULIANNE: *(A beat)* Oboe.

VADISLAV: Oboe. A very complex one, yes?

JULIANNE: Well, she's coming along.

VADISLAV: I'm sure she's wonderful.

JULIANNE: Well...

VADISLAV: Do you play?

JULIANNE: *(A beat)* Uh…no, I…

VADISLAV: Really.

JULIANNE: *(A beat, with a feigned smile…)* Well, not anymore. I played French Horn in junior high.

VADISLAV: That is another very difficult instrument.

JULIANNE: Well…

VADISLAV: Why did you stop?

JULIANNE: *(A beat, a grin of strained indulgence…)* Well, to be honest,…my horn was stolen

VADISLAV: No!

JULIANNE: Oh, yes.

VADISLAV: Oh, dear. Well, you certainly cannot say that you didn't channel your creativity into something else.

JULIANNE: Well…

VADISLAV: I used to play myself.

JULIANNE: The French horn?

VADISLAV: No, the harp.

JULIANNE: Really.

VADISLAV: A much harder instrument to steal, I must say.

JULIANNE: What made you choose the harp, if I may ask?

VADISLAV: Oh, it was not by choice. I wanted to play the trumpet, but where I'm from it is not respectable for a boy to play an instrument that is easy to transport.

JULIANNE: Really.

VADISLAV: Oh, yes.

JULIANNE: That's…certainly unusual.

VADISLAV: I'm from an unusual place. So you…

JULIANNE: *(Pleasantly taking control...)* And where is that, if I may ask?

VADISLAV: Well, these days, I am from everywhere, due to my work, but from birth; Moscow.

JULIANNE: *(Smiles, as if assumed...)* Oh, how nice.

VADISLAV: And yourself?

JULIANNE: *(A reluctant beat)* Asbury Park. New Jersey.

VADISLAV: I see, yes. And Paul?

JULIANNE: Stamford. Connecticut.

VADISLAV: Yes, I see. And you met where?

JULIANNE: *(As if uncomfortable with the pace of the questions)* In...New York.

VADISLAV: New York *City*?

JULIANNE: Mhm...

VADISLAV: The Big Apple, yes?

JULIANNE: Yes...

VADISLAV: How enchanting to meet in such a place.

JULIANNE: Hm.

VADISLAV: You were both living there at the time?

JULIANNE: Yes, we were students.

VADISLAV: I see. And then you moved here.

JULIANNE: Well, after a few years, yes...

VADISLAV: I see. And did you have family here?

JULIANNE: *(A beat...)* This *is* my family.

VADISLAV: I'm sorry, I mean your parents. Are they still in New Jersey?

JULIANNE: *(A beat, as if he's now overstepped)* Have we begun, or something?

VADISLAV: Begun what?

JULIANNE: Whatever this is?

VADISLAV: What is?

JULIANNE: Whatever you do here?

VADISLAV: Why do you ask?

JULIANNE: Well, this doesn't seem to pertain to much of anything, least of all Carrot.

VADISLAV: I'm sorry. It's just my nature to ask questions. And you are both such interesting people. I don't mean to appear intrusive.

(PAUL *enters eagerly with cordless phone...*)

PAUL: I got her! They're in the middle of a piece.

JULIANNE: Oh, Jesus Christ...

PAUL: It's okay. She was whispering. Her teacher's conducting so she has to wait for it to end. But I told her, when it's over, to tell him that she has a family emergency.

JULIANNE: She's going to tell her music teacher that *this* is a family emergency?

PAUL: I told her not to go into specifics, just that she had to be home and that she'd try to be back before rehearsals end.

JULIANNE: I really don't like this, Paul.

PAUL: (*A strained grin, as he looks at* VADISLAV...) Honey, this shouldn't take that long. She may even have time to go back. Right?

VADISLAV: We are done when we are done.

PAUL: Oh. Well,...o...okay, then...

JULIANNE: This is gonna' completely throw off her concentration.

PAUL: No, it won't. She'll be fine.

JULIANNE: Paul, have you heard her play?

PAUL: Yeah, she sounds great.

JULIANNE: She sounds *good* when she's practiced. And if she hasn't, the European judges will crucify her.

PAUL: Crucify her? Julianne, she's sixteen years old.

JULIANNE: You think they care? This is Austria, Paul, not a slumber party, for Godsakes.

PAUL: She'll be fine, okay?

JULIANNE: Paul, will you please stop saying that? You say "she'll be fine" like others blink.

PAUL: She'll... This can only benefit everyone, okay? And if we're all open to this, then I think...

VADISLAV: *(As if gently defending* JULIANNE*)* We were actually having a very nice conversation.

PAUL: Oh, you...you were?

VADISLAV: Yes. However, I know that time is of the essence so I'd like to suggest that we begin...if that is alright with everyone.

JULIANNE: *(Slight pause, then with impatience)* Fine, let's begin. Would you like to know how old he is?

VADISLAV: Your husband?

JULIANNE: Our dog.

VADISLAV: Oh, I can tell.

JULIANNE: You can tell.

VADISLAV: It's in the eyes. He is three years and possibly six months. He is a shepherd mix, even though Paul had told me he was a purebred.

PAUL: *(To* JULIANNE*)* I thought he *was* a purebred.

VADISLAV: You were misinformed.

JULIANNE: Misinformed by the animal shelter?

VADISLAV: It is not uncommon for shelters to have no concept as to the breed of a dog. But knowing the breed is not knowing the dog, you see? You can tell me that you are of German and Irish extraction, but does that mean that there is nothing more to you than sausage and leprechauns?

JULIANNE: Alright, fine. He's a mixed breed. What else would you like to know?

VADISLAV: Why don't we sit down on your lovely couch? It is much easier to conduct things this way.

PAUL: *(A beat, to* JULIANNE*)* Alright?

(A beat, before JULIANNE *goes to couch.* PAUL *follows, and sits beside her.)*

*(*VADISLAV *observes them for a considerable moment.* PAUL andJULIANNE glance at each other, *she with a certain level of unsettlement…*

VADISLAV: Hm.

(Another moment, as PAUL *and* JULIANNE *glance at each other,* PAUL *visibly more enthused. They look back at* VADISLAV.*)*

JULIANNE: Excuse me, what are you…?

VADISLAV: Please.

*(*VADISLAV *continues to observe* JULIANNE *and* PAUL *for a moment, before his phone suddenly blares "Who Let the Dogs Out"…!!!, which jolts both* JULIANNE *and* PAUL…*)*

JULIANNE / PAUL: Jesus Christ…!!! / AHHHH!!!

VADISLAV: Apologies. I will turn this off. *(He does so. He politely smiles at them, places phone back in his coat.)* Now…where were we?

JULIANNE: You were staring at us.

VADISLAV: Ah, yes. *(He resumes staring for a moment…)*

JULIANNE: This is unbelievable.

PAUL: Julianne…

JULIANNE: Can you at least ask a question? I find this very unsettling.

VADISLAV: I'm sorry. I was absorbing both of your auras.

JULIANNE: *(Slight pause)* Absorbing our auras?

VADISLAV: It aids me into knowing what to ask you? Now please. *(A beat, as he closes his eyes.)* Carrot was purchased at a shelter, you said?

JULIANNE: Yes.

VADISLAV: In town.

JULIANNE: Yes.

VADISLAV: When?

JULIANNE: About two years ago.

VADISLAV: No previous owner, to your knowledge?

JULIANNE: He was abandoned. That's all they told me.

VADISLAV: Yes. *(A beat)* He has a damaged left ear, I noticed.

JULIANNE: Yes. He had it at the shelter. They didn't know how he got it

VADISLAV: He was in a cage?

JULIANNE: Yes, he…yes.

VADISLAV: Alone or with another dog?

JULIANNE: He was alone.

VADISLAV: Were other dogs by themselves?

JULIANNE: I don't remember, exactly.

VADISLAV: *(A beat, as he rises and paces…)* What was his demeanor?

JULIANNE: His demeanor?

VADISLAV: Yes. Excited, anxious…

JULIANNE: He was calm.

VADISLAV: Calm.

JULIANNE: Yes. He was sitting calmly, looking at me.

VADISLAV: **You** picked him.

JULIANNE: Yes, I did.

VADISLAV: Were you not there?

PAUL: No, I wasn't.

VADISLAV: I see. *(To* JULIANNE*)* So *you* picked him.

JULIANNE: Yes.

VADISLAV: Because of his demeanor.

JULIANNE: Among other reasons.

VADISLAV: And what were they?

JULIANNE: I thought he was a beautiful dog. He seemed more mature than the others I'd seen…

VADISLAV: And you?

PAUL: Well, I wasn't there.

VADISLAV: But when your wife brought Carrot home, what did you feel?

PAUL: He was…calm, yes.

VADISLAV: Did you agree with your wife's selection?

PAUL: *(Slight pause)* Um, I…no, to be honest.

VADISLAV: Was there another dog which you would've preferred?

PAUL: *(Slight pause)* Um…no, there wasn't. I didn't want us to have a dog, at that point.

VADISLAV: I see. So did the behavior Carrot exhibits towards you manifest at the beginning of your relationship with him?

PAUL: It…yes, it seemed so, yes.

VADISLAV: It did.

PAUL: Well, I mean, not to this extent…

VADISLAV: To the extent of him attacking you.

PAUL: No. I mean, he would growl at me. He wouldn't come when I called him. He would resist me walking him.

VADISLAV: Well, that is of little wonder.

PAUL: What do you mean?

VADISLAV: Well, a dog, like us, wants to be wanted, of course.

PAUL: Um, yeah, that would…

VADISLAV: However, you say that you got Carrot **for** Brittany, yes.

JULIANNE: Yes.

VADISLAV: And Brittany **wanted** Carrot.

JULIANNE: She wanted a dog.

VADISLAV: She was not with you at the shelter either?

JULIANNE: No, Carrot was a surprise.

VADISLAV: A surprise.

JULIANNE: Yes.

VADISLAV: To both her and your husband.

PAUL: Yes…

JULIANNE: Paul knew I wanted to get a dog for Brittany.

PAUL: *(A forced grin)* Yes, but I didn't think she'd just go and get one on a spur of the moment.

JULIANNE: *(An equal grin…)* It wasn't a spur of the moment, honey. I told you.

PAUL: Yes, you did, but you didn't tell me you were actually going to do it. That's all I'm saying...

VADISLAV: And so...upon Brittany seeing Carrot, it is possible that she was...disappointed, yes?

JULIANNE: No, she liked him.

PAUL: Well...

JULIANNE: She did, Paul. She was a little afraid of him, but...

VADISLAV: Afraid.

JULIANNE: A little, yes. He's a large dog.

VADISLAV: Though she did say she wanted a dog.

JULIANNE: Yes, I've already said that.

VADISLAV: She did not specify the type of dog she wanted.

JULIANNE: Look, for months she'd been asking for a dog, so I got her a dog myself. There were no breed specifications.

VADISLAV: *(Slight pause, before an obliging smile)* That's fine. *(A moment, he smiles as he speaks out...)* You know, where I am from, there is a holiday called Day of the Dog. I was born on that day. I wasn't aware of its significance initially, except that on every birthday of mine, there was a parade of all the dogs through the town square. All breeds of dogs, just trotting through the street, so happy. Beaming, even. Walking in perfect harmony with one another. And from a very early age, I recall sitting atop my father's shoulders and watching them. I was struck by them and by the adulation they were receiving. I remember when I finally asked my father if *all* animals had their day. And when he said "No", I asked why,...and he said "Because dogs are special creatures. They have the greatest understanding of human behavior and yet, at the same time, they can also *absorb* it better than any other animal". *(Slight pause)* So the question I ask is…what sort of behavior exhibited in this household is *Carrot* absorbing? Why is he behaving as he is today?

JULIANNE: *(A beat, subtly offended)* Well, don't you think being abandoned would have something to do with it?

VADISLAV: Possibly.

JULIANNE: I mean, rather than question us about our "behavior", don't you think we should attribute a lot of Carrot's to the fact that he was a discarded animal? Abused? Isn't that enough to assume?

VADISLAV: Still, it is an assumption. We don't know what happened to him. All that is certain is what we know to be fact.

JULIANNE: So what are you saying? That his behavior has to result from our neglect?

VADISLAV: I'm not saying anything. I am only asking.

PAUL: *(Having pondered this throughout…)* I think Carrot senses my not wanting him,…and he hates me for it.

JULIANNE: My God, Paul…

PAUL: He does. What he's saying confirms it.

JULIANNE: He does not hate you.

PAUL: Julianne, if sending me to the emergency room doesn't qualify as hatred, I don't know what does, okay? I've always felt…hostility from him, and this feeling's only gotten more pronounced over time and so I'm…now I'm like Brittany. I've become afraid of him and so he senses my fear, and dogs respond to fear, right? Isn't…?

VADISLAV / JULIANNE: Yes, but…/ Paul, for Godsakes…

PAUL: *(Somewhat passionately…)* Yes, yes, you see?! I've heard about this stuff. That guy talks about this – the one who's on after *Ferret Frenzy*. He's responding to our fear, so what really needs to be done is that he needs to…*you* need to instill in us a…a fearless approach wherein Carrot will feel that I'm…that we're in control. That we're his…his… Whata' they call it, the pack leader, right?

(The sound of Carrot scratching against the sliding door jolts PAUL, *as before…)*

PAUL: AHHH!

JULIANNE: Paul, relax. It's just the dog.

PAUL: Yes, I know it's the dog! That's why I'm reacting fearfully!

JULIANNE: Do not snap at me, Paul.

PAUL: I'm sorry, I just…

VADISLAV: *(To* JULIANNE*)* Have you noticed your husband's reactions before?

JULIANNE: *(Absurdly…)* On occasion, yes…

VADISLAV: On occasion.

JULIANNE: Yes, so what does that say?

VADISLAV: Well, I've only been here a half an hour and I've noticed this reaction twice already.

JULIANNE: Well, I'm often with clients. I'm not always home, and when I am, we're not always in the same room.

VADISLAV: Understood.

JULIANNE: And, frankly, I think Paul chooses to be a little dramatic.

PAUL: How can you say that? This dog looks at me, it's like he's staring at a pot roast.

JULIANNE: Paul, Carrot is not some wild grizzly. I've said this before; he gets nervous, and if you're nervous around him, he probably picks up on that and that exacerbates the situation.

VADISLAV: That's a very good observation.

JULIANNE: Thank you.

VADISLAV: *(To* PAUL*)* So you would prefer not to deal with him.

PAUL: I...well, I mean, with him as he is now, no, but...

VADISLAV: And yet you *do* deal with him.

PAUL: I...well, I try...

VADISLAV: *(To* JULIANNE*)* Because *you* ask him to.

JULIANNE: When I'm not home, there's not much of a choice. Even if I could take Carrot with me everywhere, he gets car sick.

VADISLAV: He does.

JULIANNE: Yes, he does. Anyway, Carrot belongs to everyone in this house. Not just me.

VADISLAV: Well, that is immaterial.

JULIANNE: What is immaterial?

VADISLAV: Dogs are not stuffed toys. They do not understand the concept of *belonging* to anyone. They gravitate towards who they gravitate to. In this case, you, yes?

PAUL: Yes.

JULIANNE: *(While looking at* PAUL*...)* Alright, but...

VADISLAV: Can one say that he has considerable affection for you?

PAUL: Yes.

JULIANNE: Honey, will you let me speak?

PAUL: Well, he does...

JULIANNE: Paul, if I'm going to sit here, at the very least you can let me answer a question that I'm being asked.

VADISLAV: That is true. Please, let her respond.

JULIANNE: Thank you. Yes, you can say that he does.

VADISLAV: So let's say that.

JULIANNE: I just said it.

VADISLAV: Yes, you did.

JULIANNE: So it's my fault.

VADISLAV: No, no one is saying any such thing. After all, you did select him. It was you who first set eyes upon him. It is you who rescued him from what may have very well been a certain death. It is you who seemingly wanted him in the first place so, at the very least, it only makes sense that he would favor you, especially if there has never been a true willingness on anyone else's part to accept him. *(To* PAUL*)* Yes?

PAUL: *(Somewhat guiltily)* I...well...

VADISLAV: I mean, *you* certainly did not, did you.

PAUL: I...yes, I suppose that's true...

VADISLAV: Well, you've said it, yes? I'm not putting words into your mouth.

PAUL: No, not at...

VADISLAV: You did not want a dog.

PAUL: Yes, I...yes, that's right.

VADISLAV: Okay, then. And why is that?

PAUL: *(Slight pause)* Because...we already had Wolfgang.

VADISLAV: *(A beat)* Wolfgang?

PAUL: Yes.

VADISLAV: Who is that?

PAUL: *(Pause)* It was our cat.

(Lights out)

END OF ACT ONE

ACT TWO

(The scene resumes in response to the last line from ACT ONE...)

VADISLAV: *(Slight pause)* Your cat.

PAUL: Yes.

VADISLAV: *(Pondering)* Therefore, your feeling was that to get a dog at the same time that you already had a cat would not be wise?

PAUL: Yes.

VADISLAV: It wasn't that you simply did not want a dog.

PAUL: No. No, not at all.

VADISLAV: I see.

PAUL: I mean, we'd gotten Wolfgang for Brittany about three years ago and I just...I felt that she should just, you know, have the one pet. Appreciate him.

VADISLAV: And did she?

JULIANNE: Yes, she did. Now can we...?

PAUL: Oh, God, yeah. Brittany loved Wolfgang. He'd follow her throughout the house, sleep with her, lie on her homework. It was very cute, actually.

VADISLAV: It sounds as if you had a good relationship with him as well.

PAUL: *(With restrained pride…)* Yes, I did. He'd always jump on the counter when I was preparing dinner. I'd let him sit and watch me, give him little samples. He really loved my cooking.

VADISLAV: I see.

PAUL: He really seemed to admire me, y'know? It was as if…

JULIANNE: Honey.

PAUL: What?

JULIANNE: You're digressing.

PAUL: Well, he's asking why I didn't want a dog, and I'm giving him a reason…

JULIANNE: Yes, and you did that.

PAUL: I mean, I don't want it to seem like I'm this cold bastard who just hates dogs…

JULIANNE: Nobody thinks that, Paul. Now let's move on, okay? I don't have all day.

PAUL: *(Slight pause, to VADISLAV…)* Sorry,…I just… It's a very sore subject with me, that's all.

VADISLAV: Sore because…Wolfgang is no longer here?

PAUL: *(Slight pause, suddenly emotional…)* Because… *(He quickly rises, while masking his tears with his hand…)* Excuse me. I'll be right…

(PAUL urgently exits off. A beat, before JULIANNE impatiently rises…)

JULIANNE: Alright, I think we've had enough lines of questioning for today. Would you like to see the dog?

VADISLAV: I've seen the dog.

JULIANNE: I mean, would you like to do what you've been hired to do?

VADISLAV: This **is** what I've been hired to do.

JULIANNE: Excuse me, my husband is off sobbing in the bathroom. I'd say that's a little counterproductive.

VADISLAV: I'm sorry, but expressions of emotion are not necessarily an adverse result of what I do. Evidently, I've tapped into something.

JULIANNE: The cat ran away, okay? That's what he's reacting to.

VADISLAV: I see.

JULIANNE: So what does that have to do with why you're here? You're a *Canine* Relations Specialist, right?

VADISLAV: Yes, I am.

JULIANNE: Well, I've yet to see you *relate* in any way to a canine, other than Paul telling me that you made some hand signal through the sliding doors, which is probably nothing more than a parlor trick anyway.

VADISLAV: I assure you that…

JULIANNE: With all due respect, Vadislav, I don't care, alright? My husband has obviously lost the handle on this issue, so I will take it upon myself to oversee things here, okay? Now would you like to help our dog?

VADISLAV: I'm afraid that is not how this works…

JULIANNE: Alright, then I'm afraid we're done here. Thank you for your time.

VADISLAV: I'm sorry to hear that.

JULIANNE: And we're not paying you for this either.

VADISLAV: For what?

JULIANNE: For whatever this was.

VADISLAV: What was? I didn't do anything.

JULIANNE: You…that's… Yes, that's right. So I'm just making that clear before I leave the room and Paul ends up baking you a quiche and writing you a check.

VADISLAV: I wouldn't accept it if he did. I'll even pay you.

JULIANNE: For what?

VADISLAV: For the sandwich and the vodka. These are expensive items, I'm aware. I didn't come here for a free meal.

JULIANNE: No, that's not… Just, please, leave, alright?

(…as PAUL enters…)

PAUL: What's going on?

JULIANNE: Paul, really, we're done with this. I'm calling Brittany back.

PAUL: Julianne…

JULIANNE: No, Paul, that's it. We've been indulgent enough.

PAUL: Julianne,… Look, Vadislav, can you just show her your license…

JULIANNE: I've already seen his Goddamn license, Paul. Jesus, he coulda' made it himself, for Godsakes.

PAUL: Why are you being so resistant about this?

JULIANNE: I am resistant to *him*, Paul, because his practices are disturbing to me.

PAUL: He's asking questions.

JULIANNE: He's asking questions that're sending you off crying in the bathroom.

PAUL: It's not his fault. It's how I responded, Julianne…

JULIANNE: Paul, please…

PAUL: It's therapeutic.

JULIANNE: It's therapeutic if you're in *therapy*. When you're dealing with a Canine Relations Specialist, it's ridiculous and invasive.

PAUL: Julianne...

VADISLAV: *(Very gingerly)* I know there is some resistance to me at the moment, but if I may interject here...

JULIANNE: *(Over "...here...")* Yes?!

VADISLAV: May I use your bathroom again, please?

PAUL / JULIANNE: Sure, you... / Absolutely not...

PAUL: Julianne, that's not very hospitable...

JULIANNE: *(To VADISLAV)* There is a Chevron station five minutes from here, alright? You can use their facilities. *(To PAUL)* I can't believe you're doing this to me on the most important day of my career...

PAUL: Julianne, I'm not doing anything to you. This is *for* all of us...

JULIANNE: This is not for anybody, Paul...

PAUL: Julianne...

JULIANNE: I was skeptical about this from the moment he said for us to pull our daughter out of rehearsal, okay?

PAUL: Jul...

JULIANNE: Now I will take the reins and deal with this situation, despite the enormity of my schedule, because I am not going to allow this family to turn their lives upside down because of this man.

(As VADISLAV gathers handbag...)

VADISLAV: You don't have to do anything. This is a free country.

PAUL / JULIANNE: No, Vadislav, please… / I'm aware…!

PAUL: *(Almost desperately…)* Vadislav, please, I need you to stay.

JULIANNE: Paul…

PAUL: I'm sorry, she's… This is a very special day in her career and all but I'm hoping she'll come around…

JULIANNE: How dare you? "Come around"?!

PAUL: Julianne…

JULIANNE: What, am **I** a dog now?!

PAUL: I didn't mean…

JULIANNE: I am who I am, and that is not someone who's gonna' allow themselves to be manipulated.

PAUL: Julianne, I'm not being manipulated…

JULIANNE: *(Over "manipulated…")* I mean, what do you suppose will happen if I don't intercede now, Paul? If I let him walk all over you, have him pull Brittany out of practice, bomb in Austria because she's already under rehearsed…?

PAUL: That's not…

JULIANNE: *Her confidence will be irreparably shot!*

PAUL: *(Slight pause. Containing)* I have Brittany's best interest at heart in every way, and would hope that you know that, Julianne. And I am not being manipulated here, okay? This is something that I have willed. Alright? This was a decision that I've made.

JULIANNE: This isn't a decision. It's irrational.

PAUL: Irrational?! Look at me, my God…

JULIANNE: *(Over "my God…")* It's irrational that you would endure what a stranger is putting us through in our own house.

PAUL: This is part of his method of…

JULIANNE: What method? He hasn't demonstrated anything other than that he likes your tuna fish and needs to use the Goddamn bathroom.

PAUL: I believe he can help us. Okay? I wouldn't go through this if I didn't feel that…

JULIANNE: Well, I don't, okay? I have an uncomfortable feeling about what is transpiring here and, if I feel this way in my own home, Paul, then something is awry, do you understand?

PAUL: Nothing is awry, Julianne…

JULIANNE: *(Over "Julianne…")* Paul, I do not want to continue this discussion, especially in the presence of a complete…

PAUL: *(Over "presence of…")* Julianne, I've hired this man because I am concerned for the safety and well-being of this household. I've committed to this like I haven't committed to anything in years, because if I don't, this dog may very well devour two thirds of this family.

JULIANNE: That's insanity.

PAUL: Julianne, have you noticed these bandages? I look like I've been in combat. And if it wasn't for me throwing myself in front of him, God knows what he'd do to Brittany.

JULIANNE: Paul, do not even imply that Carrot would…!

PAUL: I've seen it, Julianne! I've been here when it's looked like he was gonna'…!

(The phone rings!)

JULIANNE: Give me that phone.

(PAUL retrieves it, and withholds it…)

PAUL: Julianne, please…

JULIANNE: Is that her? Give me that phone, Paul. If it's Brittany, I'm telling her to stay at rehearsal.

PAUL: Julianne…

JULIANNE: Paul, give me that phone…!

PAUL: JULIANNE, I'M HANDLING THIS, OKAY?!!! *(Nearly trembling…)* If you don't want to be a part of this, fine, but Brittany is coming home regardless of what her stupid band teacher says, *and this man is staying!*

(JULIANNE is stricken momentarily by this, before PAUL finally picks up…)

PAUL: *(An animatedly gentle tone…)* Hello? —Hi, honey. —He said it's okay? —Good —I think this is really gonna' work. —No, I…I don't think so. I really think it'll work, sweetie. —So…what do you think, like a half hour? —Okay. We'll see you then. Bye, swee… Hello? *(A beat, clicks off phone.)*

VADISLAV: Is she alright?

PAUL: *(A strained though elaborate smile)* Oh, yes. She's fine. Her music teacher said it's fine. She'll just have to practice extra tonight. And they'll have time when there in Austria, before they perform.

VADISLAV: I see.

PAUL: *(Slight pause, to VADISLAV)* She's looking forward to this.

VADISLAV: Is she?

PAUL: Well,…no, she seems a little tenuous about it, actually, but…she's coming, so…

VADISLAV: Well, that counts for something.

PAUL: Yes, it sure does. Yes.

(VADISLAV *observes both for a moment, as* PAUL *strains to keep his best face on, while* JULIANNE *seethes, looking out.*)

PAUL: Is everything alright?

VADISLAV: *(Slight pause)* I'm sorry. It just dawned on me.

PAUL: What?

VADISLAV: Perhaps Carrot is merely being protective. *(To* JULIANNE*)* Of *you.*

PAUL: I...well, yeah, that's certainly... I mean, he was abandoned and, as you said, she did pick him out...

VADISLAV: I mean, with things as they are within your household. Demonstrative behavior. *(Slight pause)* Perhaps something more.

PAUL: *(A beat)* I...what, I'm sorry. What do you mean, exactly?

VADISLAV: *(Slight pause)* Does your husband abuse you?

PAUL: What?!

VADISLAV: It is a question.

PAUL: You've gotta' be... No, I don't abuse her. What kind of a question is that?

VADISLAV: There have been times, in my experience, where an animal's irregular or volatile behavior stemmed from violence within the home. And it was only through my questioning that the spouse had the courage to save themselves from further abuse.

PAUL: Well, I'm sorry, Voslav...

VADISLAV: Vadislav.

PAUL: Vadislav, but no one has abused anyone except that dog, I can assure you.

VADISLAV: There is no need to get defensive if there is no guilt.

PAUL: I'm…I'm not! I'm not getting defensive. I'm just saying that I haven't abused my wife.

VADISLAV: This is not an accusation. A situation has many sides. I'm simply assessing the possibilities.

PAUL: *(A stunned snicker…)* Well, that's…I'm sorry, but that's not one, alright?

(PAUL observes JULIANNE, who is taken slightly aback, as though this question has touched upon something, however related or unrelated…)

PAUL: Julianne, can you… Can you tell him that I have never laid a hand on you in a violent manner, please?

VADISLAV: Is that true?

PAUL: Yes, it's…

VADISLAV: I'm asking your wife.

PAUL: *(Suddenly feeling betrayed)* I'm sorry. Fine. Tell him so we can move on here, please.

JULIANNE: Don't tell me what to say.

PAUL: I'm…Ju…, I'm not. What, am I putting words in your mouth?

VADISLAV: You do have that tendency.

PAUL: I…what? I can't believe this. Vadislav, how…? *(A beat)* Julianne…?

(A moment)

JULIANNE: *(Not to anyone, with residual humiliation)* My husband has never laid a violent hand on me.

PAUL: Thank you. There you go, okay?

VADISLAV: I'm glad to hear it.

JULIANNE: *(Almost subconsciously)* He hasn't touched me in *any* way in some time.

VADISLAV: Oh. Well. Hello!

PAUL: *(A stunned moment, to* JULIANNE*)* Why...why would you say such a thing?

JULIANNE: Because it's true.

PAUL: It's not... Alri... Who cares if it's true? This is not about our sex life.

JULIANNE: He asked.

PAUL: I didn't hear him ask that. Did you ask that?

VADISLAV: Whether I did or not, it's certainly interesting to hear.

PAUL: *(To* JULIANNE*)* Well,...you didn't have to respond with such a thing.

JULIANNE: Oh, *now* this is embarrassing for you?

PAUL: My God, a minute ago you're kicking this man out of our house and now you're divulging this sordid information to him?

JULIANNE: You've "willed" this situation, right? You want to be responsible for this? Fine. With what time I have to spare, I'll indulge you, Paul.

(A still moment, with PAUL *obviously taken aback.)*

*(*VADISLAV *observes with a cordial smile, while* JULIANNE *maintains her resentment.)*

VADISLAV: May we resume?

(Indicating, ever cordially, that they resume their places on the couch. JULIANNE *slowly does so.* PAUL *observes her, before following in the same fashion.)*

(A beat)

*(*VADISLAV *sits before* JULIANNE *and* PAUL, *and, as before, observes them for a moment.)*

VADISLAV: You are a very attractive couple.

PAUL: *(Slight pause)* Well, that's...I...thank...thank you.

VADISLAV: A very nice looking pair. It is surprising that you don't have relations anymore. Though I suppose there are always reasons that are certainly none of my beeswax, as they say.

PAUL: Well...

VADISLAV: *(A beat)* Marriage is a very complex union. And yet it is the center of why the earth is what it is, isn't it? People meet, they marry, they have offspring, the cycle continues and through that we have our ever-evolving planet. At least ideally, yes? Divorce has become so rampant in this country. It's very disappointing. And largely because men and women grow to find that they no longer find each other attractive. Maybe because they find they know each other too well, or not really at all. And once they've come to that realization, rather than attempt to rectify it,...they give up. And so the marital foundation begins to crack...and there is nowhere for the family to stand. And the children slip through. And that is a shame. *(Slight pause, proudly)* My parents were married for eighty-one years. Isn't that something?

PAUL: *(Slight pause)* Wow, that's...yes...

VADISLAV: Eighty-one years. They had their children. We grew up well, went our ways, and they stayed together. Loved each other. And remained together until their deaths.

PAUL: Well, that's...that's...uh...really beautiful.

VADISLAV: Well, not as beautiful as one would hope. One week after their eighty-first anniversary, my parents had their throats cut by burglars. But, had they had a dog, it would have made all the difference, I feel. I had always told them*"get a watch dog"*, but... Anyway, my point is that, up until then, they had bliss. And now, I believe they have *eternal* bliss. The important thing is to not give up. To be willing to succeed. And the same goes with Carrot. If you believe that the "problems" can be rectified, they will. And you will have bliss within your household.

(VADISLAV *smiles at them with utter sincerity, ...while* PAUL *grins weakly at* JULIANNE *who, in turn, sustains her hostility towards him.*)

(*After a beat,* VADISLAV *rises...*)

VADISLAV: Now, if you don't mind, might you provide me with directions to your Chevron station?

PAUL: I'm sorry?

VADISLAV: I'm afraid if I withhold my fluid much longer, I may suffer a bladder infection.

PAUL: (*Rises...*) Oh. Oh, I'm... No, please, use our... Julianne, Vadislav can... It's okay, right?

JULIANNE: (*Slight pause, quietly piercing*) Why are you asking *me*?

PAUL: (*A resentful pause, while looking at* JULIANNE) Alright. Vadislav, please, use our bathroom, alright?

VADISLAV: You're certain? I...

PAUL: *I'm positive.*

VADISLAV: Very well. Thank you both. (*He goes off.*)

(JULIANNE *remains sitting, containing obvious bitterness and humiliation, while* PAUL'S *momentary façade of bravado has subtly evaporated. He attempts to avoid eye contact, while she looks out.*)

PAUL: This is...a little strange alluvasudden, isn't it? I'm... (*Slight pause*) That's...that's really shocking about his parents, huh? How...unfortunate. (*He bides his time awkwardly roaming and touching furniture, as if he were a stranger in his own house...before looking at her...*) I really wish you didn't say what you said. I mean, where did that...? I'm sorry if I raised my voice but, I mean...you

didn't need to... *(Then, with sudden enthusiasm.)* This...
this is going to be an enormously positive experience
if you just...let it, okay? Just trust that my instincts
on this are right this time, ...okay? *(Slight pause)* And
when you need to get ready for your meeting, you do
what you have to do. I know how important that is to
you. To all of us, of course. Brittany'll be here soon,
and we'll...everything'll... Okay? *(Slight pause)* Ju...
Okay?

JULIANNE: *(Slight pause)* I think I know what this is
doing for you now.

PAUL: What do you mean?

JULIANNE: Sure, this man comes from a testosterone
dominated culture, one where I'm sure women can
barely *speak*, let alone have a career, and you're feeding
off it.

PAUL: Julianne, I'm not letting him influence...

JULIANNE: You just felt that you needed to put me in
my place?

PAUL: I...no, Julianne...

JULIANNE: Well, what is yelling at me in front of a
stranger supposed to represent then?

PAUL: I didn't mean to yell...

JULIANNE: That may be the way they do things
where *he's* from, Paul, but here, in this house, that is
chauvinistic bullshit.

PAUL: I didn't mean to yell at you, okay? You were
just...not allowing me to handle this...

JULIANNE: Paul, for Godsakes, I was trying to protect
you.

PAUL: Protect me?

JULIANNE: Yes.

PAUL: From what?

JULIANNE: From what? From subjecting yourself to further embarrassment?

PAUL: What...? The only thing I've been embarrassed by is what you said.

JULIANNE: What *I* said?

PAUL: *(A slightly hushed tone)* About our *sex* life? What the hell was that?

JULIANNE: *(Turning out...)* I thought it was relevant.

PAUL: You were being spiteful.

JULIANNE: He asked a question, Paul...

PAUL: He didn't ask *that*.

JULIANNE: Paul, I responded in accordance with how I felt at that moment, okay? Was I hurt? Was I humiliated? You're damn right, and I was entitled to that. I mean, Jesus, is it anymore unnecessary than you going on a tangent about how the cat used to "admire" you?

PAUL: *That* was relevant!

JULIANNE: It wasn't relevant. This is about the dog.

PAUL: Well, we had a cat before we had a dog and because of the dog, we don't have a cat. That is relevant.

JULIANNE: Carrot is not the reason, Paul...

PAUL: Julianne...

JULIANNE: Don't you dare insinuate...

PAUL: Julianne, I'm not insinuating...

JULIANNE: *(Over "insinuating...")* Paul, do not...

PAUL: *Carrot ate Wolfgang!*

JULIANNE: *(A beat)* He did not eat him, Paul. The cat ran away. You know this.

PAUL: I don't know that, Julianne. I've never known that.

JULIANNE: *(Slight pause)* Well, *this* is new.

PAUL: All I know is that Wolfgang's collar was in Carrot's stool.

JULIANNE: Yes, his *collar*, Paul! His collar was probably loose and came off somehow. He coulda' removed it himself. Cats are like magicians that way.

PAUL: His collar wouldn't just come off like that. And he liked that collar. It had his name on it and everything.

JULIANNE: Wolfgang didn't know his name was on his collar.

PAUL: Even so, he wouldn't't've taken it off...

JULIANNE: Paul, they're animals. They have instincts. Cats are curious, right? He could've seen a bird and hopped the fence. He'd done it before. Any number of things could've happened.

PAUL: Well, Carrot's an animal. And he's a dog. And dogs usually hate cats. And he didn't seem to care for Wolfgang. So don't you think that it's a least a possibility...?

JULIANNE: *(Over "possibility...")* Carrot did not kill the Goddamn cat, Paul!!!

(A moment)

PAUL: Yeah, well,...what does it matter to you anyway, right?

JULIANNE: *(Slight pause)* What does *that* mean?

PAUL: You didn't even like him.

JULIANNE: *(Slight pause)* What?

PAUL: Ever since that time you pet him too hard and he swiped at your hand. That was it. You never forgave him for that.

JULIANNE: *(Slight pause)* My God, you don't even know me.

PAUL: Alright, I didn't mean…

JULIANNE: How dare you insinuate that I somehow willed the cat's disappearance…

PAUL: Julianne…

JULIANNE: Who the hell do you think you are…?

PAUL: I'm not saying that it's your fault…

JULIANNE: Saying that I didn't like Wolfgang is making me at fault for his disappearance, Paul.

PAUL: It's not…

JULIANNE: You're equating my not smothering the cat like you did with the cat not being here. One thing has nothing to do with the other and it's appalling for you to even suggest it.

PAUL: You're right, okay? I didn't mean…

JULIANNE: So what if I wasn't enamored with Wolfgang. That doesn't mean I wished him gone.

PAUL: I know…

JULIANNE: And so I have a good relationship with Carrot, so that makes us co-conspirators?

PAUL: No, not at…

JULIANNE: Why did I always feed Wolfgang, even if he preferred your cooking? Why did I always make sure the shade of his favorite window was open if I was the first to leave in the morning so that he could bathe in the sun, right up until the day he vanished?

PAUL: *(Attempting to calm her…)* Okay, Julianne…

JULIANNE: *(Over "Julianne…")* Just like why did I choose to lose a high-paying client to bandage you up and spend the night in the Emergency room….?

PAUL: I didn't ask for that, Julianne…

JULIANNE: That's right. You didn't ask. I took it upon myself.

PAUL: And I thanked you.

JULIANNE: I'm not asking for your thanks, Paul.

PAUL: Then…I don't know what you want here…

JULIANNE: I'm saying that I'm not the devious, self-centered bitch you're portraying me as.

PAUL: Julianne, I'm not saying…

JULIANNE: You're suggesting it, Paul, and it's unfair. And just because you're responsible for hiring this man does not make you some martyr.

PAUL: *(A beat)* You're here. And I appreciate it. Okay?

JULIANNE: *(Slight pause, hurt)* Tsch. You make it sound as if I'm doing community service, for Godsakes…

PAUL: Jesus, Julianne…

JULIANNE: *I'm still a part of this family!*

PAUL: *(Slight pause, taken aback)* I never said you weren't.

(JULIANNE looks resentfully at PAUL.)

(A moment, before PAUL takes a few aimless steps away from JULIANNE.)

PAUL: He's…he's going to come back soon, so let's… Can we just…? I'm sure he won't need you much longer.

JULIANNE: Sure, you'll be glad to get *me* out of the room.

PAUL: Julianne, please…

JULIANNE: I'll be off pitching my heart out for the sake of our financial well-being, to help pay for the car that you insisted on getting our daughter for her 16th birthday, while you and her make me out to be Stalin.

PAUL: Julianne, don't say such a thing…!

JULIANNE: Like you don't already.

PAUL: What the hell are you talking…?

JULIANNE: Gee, I wonder if *Brittany* thinks Carrot ate Wolfgang.

PAUL: Julianne, stop it…!

JULIANNE: Of course, God forbid a gift I give her would simply be appreciated…

PAUL: She did, Julianne, but the dog scares her. She's practically afraid to come in the house…!

JULIANNE: I'm sick of you telling me how my daughter feels, Paul!

PAUL: *(Slight pause, an empty consolation)* It's not like she talks to *me* much anymore either.

JULIANNE: *(A beat, as if a nerve)* Oh, is that so.

PAUL: What the hell does *that* mean?

JULIANNE: *(Slight pause, looks at* PAUL*)* You don't know?

PAUL: Know what?

*(*JULIANNE *continues to look at* PAUL *bitterly, before turning out.)*

JULIANNE: *(A beat, as she looks out.)* So I suppose you attribute her behavior to *Carrot*, right?

PAUL: *(A beat)* It hasn't helped, I'll say that. But also…I mean, she's, y'know, she's a teenager. She's probably going through stuff that she can't verbalize. I'm sure we went through it, to some degree…

JULIANNE: Speak for yourself, Paul.

PAUL: Okay, I'll speak for myself.

JULIANNE: What I went through, you or she wouldn't be able to fathom.

PAUL: Yes, I know...

JULIANNE: I was raised by fucking wolves.

PAUL: I know...

JULIANNE: You think they would even *think* of getting me a dog? They would've sooner *eaten* one!

PAUL: *(Pause, a careful breath)* I'm glad that you're willing to contribute here, okay? I mean,...there's no other way it should be. It's like Vadislav said, this concerns the family, right? And we're...you're... Okay? *(Slight pause)* And I'm sorry that I hurt you, Julianne. *(Slight pause, more to himself)* I didn't know I could.

JULIANNE: *(Slight pause, softly)* You didn't...? Okay, Paul.

PAUL: I'm not being flippant about it...

JULIANNE: No, I understand. You didn't know,...and now you do. *(She remains sitting, looking out, and soon begins to internally weep...)*

(PAUL takes notice of this, and is hesitant to approach JULIANNE...)

PAUL: Ju...? Honey, are you...?

JULIANNE: I'm fine.

(A moment, before PAUL eventually sits beside JULIANNE, but at a distinct distance. He appears as if he is close to, in some way, consoling her, but is visibly unable to follow through...)

(After a moment of JULIANNE's emotional restraint, she abruptly rises...)

JULIANNE: Jesus Christ!

PAUL: What?

JULIANNE: Can't you just…can't you just…?

PAUL: What? I don't…

JULIANNE: What is it to just put your arm around me, for Godsakes?!

PAUL: I didn't know …I wasn't sure that's what you…

JULIANNE: What's to know?! You just do it, Paul!

PAUL: Well, my God, you don't make it easy.

JULIANNE: I don't.

PAUL: I'm gonna' put my arm around you *now*? It'll be like embracing a porcupine.

JULIANNE: Boy, you're just really in form today, aren't you. How nice.

PAUL: *(Over "How nice.")* Jesus Christ, I wanted…you saw me come over to you. It's not like I'm oblivious…

JULIANNE: *(Over "oblivious…")* How long have we been together, Paul?

PAUL: Julianne…

JULIANNE: I'm asking…

PAUL: It doesn't matter how long. Does it?

JULIANNE: It doesn't matter?

PAUL: *(Slight pause)* I mean, things've…changed, y'know?

JULIANNE: *(Slight pause, pierced by this)* I know they have, Paul, but, for Godsakes, we are still… I mean, don't you have the instinct to just…to just…? We'd barely said a word to each other for days. But the day I heard that bloodcurdling yell, I came running out to you…because something takes over. Even if things aren't like they were, something takes over because… You can't just… Or maybe you can. Maybe I should to.

PAUL: I would've done the same for you.

JULIANNE: Really.

PAUL: How can you question that?

JULIANNE: Because things have "changed".

PAUL: Jesus Christ, there's not a phrase or a sentence I utter that you don't throw right back in my face...

JULIANNE: *(Over "...in my face...")* I'm just agreeing with you.

PAUL: Maybe it'd be nice if you just respected me a little more, like you used to. Y'know, I can't help it if I didn't have your childhood, Julianne. I was only screwed up *mentally*, okay? If I could, believe me, I'd dig up my father from the grave and have him beat the living shit out of me...

JULIANNE: How can you say something like that...?

PAUL: *(Over "something like that...")* I'm saying you can apologize to *me*, y'know? *I've* been hurt. *I've* been humiliated. *I've* overcome stuff. My God, it was all I could do to step into a kitchen to make *toast* after what happened to me in New York, but I did.

JULIANNE: I went back to work and I needed help in the house.

PAUL: And I did more than help.

JULIANNE: Yes, you took it upon yourself to cook exclusively, Paul. I've never denied that.

PAUL: I did more than that, Julianne, and you know it...

JULIANNE: Fine, you did everything.

PAUL: No, I didn't do *"everything"*, I did *things*, okay?! *Many* things, including providing nourishment for my family. You know, back in the day when we actually

sat down as a family. Back when you actually let
Brittany eat.

JULIANNE: When I *let* her eat?

PAUL: You got her thinking she's overweight, so now
we're lucky if she has a radish for dinner. She's gonna'
be thinner than her oboe soon.

JULIANNE: I never said she was overweight.

PAUL: You said that...

JULIANNE: I said that she has the "potential" to be
overweight.

PAUL: Well, what the hell is that? Everyone has the
potential to be anything, but you say "overweight" to a
sixteen year old and, before you know it, she's Karen
Carpenter.

JULIANNE: Oh, so now I've made Brittany bulimic?!

PAUL: No, but she sure has the "potential", doesn't
she?

JULIANNE: Boy, this really **is** what this is all about.

PAUL: What...?

JULIANNE: This isn't about Carrot. It's about getting
some big Russian guy inspiring you to say these
terrible things to me that you've never had the
audacity to say before.

PAUL: That couldn't be further...

JULIANNE: Bullshit! I bet the only reason you didn't
say this shit to me when we were in counseling was
because our counselor was a small Indian woman.

PAUL: I had no idea what this was gonna' turn into. I
just wanted help with the dog.

JULIANNE: I'm sure.

PAUL: And it's not like he's siding with me. For Godsakes, you got him to think that I *abuse* you, remember? God knows what he thinks now.

JULIANNE: I didn't "get him" to think anything, Paul. You gave him that impression. I didn't say a damn thing.

PAUL: Alright, fine! Let's just say it's *all* my fault, okay?! It's my fault that we can't have a simple dinner as a family! It's my fault if I move a vase two inches to the left so as to disrupt the "domestic chi".

(…as PAUL moves vase…)

JULIANNE: Paul, stop this…

PAUL: It's all me, Julianne. It's my fault that we don't have SEX!

JULIANNE: PAUL!

PAUL: It's my fault that the dog won't let me come within a five foot radius of you without going for my throat. It's my fault that, when you're not working, you're always *walking the dog*, or *playing with the dog* or *talking to the dog*…!

JULIANNE: *Someone* has to give him some attention. You and Brittany completely avoid him!

PAUL: That's because we **fear** him!!!

JULIANNE: You never wanted him and that's why we have this. *Even Vadislav said it!* That's why we're in this situation in the first place.

PAUL: He didn't say it was my fault. He said he was assessing the possibilities.

JULIANNE: Yeah, well, at least he appreciates your cooking, right?

PAUL: What does that…?

JULIANNE: If he ultimately deems you at fault for Carrot's behavior, you'll turn him around with a Bundt cake and then it'll be *my* fault again.

PAUL: Jesus Christ, this isn't about *blame,* Julianne...!

JULIANNE: *Then what is it about, Paul?!!!* Because all I know is that we have a "Canine Relations Specialist" who hasn't so much as glanced at our dog sitting on my toilet for a disturbingly long time now and I have become *gravely* unsettled by it!

(As Carrot begins to scratch and growl in tune with JULIANNE'S *volume...)*

PAUL: Alright, I'll...

JULIANNE: What the hell is he doing in there, retiling?!

PAUL: I'll check in on him, okay? Just...

JULIANNE: What kind of person uses a guest bathroom for this long?

PAUL: I will check in on him, okay...?!

JULIANNE: *(Over " okay...?!")* Then do it, please! Enough is enough already.

(A moment, as JULIANNE *looks at* PAUL *awaiting his departure. After a moment,* PAUL *reluctantly goes off...)*

(Carrot continues to scratch the sliding door, along with an occasion growl, an occasional whine, a bark, etc...)

JULIANNE: Poor thing...

*(*JULIANNE *goes off. The sliding door opening is heard, which ceases the growling and barking.)*

(Throughout the following, there is a fleeting knock and a vague though unintelligible utterance from PAUL *[also off].)*

(A high-pitched, animated tone:)

JULIANNE: What a good boy. I know. I know, you're a good boy, aren't you? Aren't you? You're a good boy? Are you a good boy? Huh? Are you a good boy, Carrot? Huh? Yes, that's right. Yes. What a good boy. What a good boy. What a good boy. Yes. Yes, that's right. Were you drinking out of your fountain? Huh? Did you drink from your Buddhist fountain? Good boy. What a good boy you are.

(PAUL *eventually comes out, in the midst of the above. He waits tentatively while* JULIANNE *continues to baby talk Carrot, before motioning towards her.*)

PAUL: Um, he's…

(*However, as soon as* PAUL *is off, …a sudden, intense growl is heard from Carrot, prompting him to literally jump back into view.*)

JULIANNE: (*Off*) Carrot, no! You stop that!

(*Carrot ceases his growling.*)

PAUL: Um, Julianne, he's…Vadislav'll be out shortly. He apologizes for the delay.

JULIANNE: (*Off*) What?

PAUL: He'll be out in a bit. He apologizes. You should put Carrot outside now, okay?

JULIANNE: (*Off*) I'll put him out when I'm ready to, Paul. The poor thing's been kept outside long enough today.

PAUL: It's just…he doesn't want to see the…

JULIANNE: (*Off*) *I know, Paul!*

(PAUL *takes a moment, before aimlessly stepping about the living area. He even rehearses a forced smile of nonchalance, before discarding the attempt. Throughout this, we hear…*)

JULIANNE: (*Off*) Okay. Mommy's gonna' let you go by the pool, okay? You wana' go outside? Okay? You wana' go outside? Yes. Yes. I love you, my dear. I love you. Yes, I do. Alright, here we go, okay? Here, go get your rawhide. Go get... Good boy!

(The sliding door closes, and JULIANNE *re-enters living area, as if the offstage voice were another person. She looks at* PAUL, *with residual tension from prior.)*

JULIANNE: Where is he, Paul?

PAUL: He's coming. I just spoke to him.

*(*JULIANNE *looks at watch, ill at ease.* PAUL, *similar to before, attempts to put his best face on.)*

PAUL: When do you have to call them?

JULIANNE: *(Slight pause)* Forty-five minutes.

(An awkward moment, before JULIANNE *notices vase that* PAUL *has moved slightly. She places it exactly where it was prior.)*

(Another moment, as JULIANNE *remains with arms folded.* PAUL, *still and unsettled...)*

PAUL: He's...he's not from Russia, by the way.

JULIANNE: *(Slight pause, unclear)* What do you mean?

PAUL: Well, I'm just... You said before that he was this big "Russian" guy but, not that it matters but, just so you know, he's not.

JULIANNE: *(Pause, recalling now)* Well, *that* can't be.

PAUL: I know, he definitely seems to have a very similar accent but...

JULIANNE: No, he told me that he was.

PAUL: That he was from Russia?

JULIANNE: Well, Moscow, I mean, hello.

PAUL: *(Slight pause)* Are you sure...?

JULIANNE: Yes, I'm sure.

PAUL: *(Slight pause)* Well, that's...odd.

JULIANNE: Why?

PAUL: *(A beat)* I asked him if he was from Russia and he distinctly said no.

JULIANNE: *(A beat)* Are you sure?

PAUL: Yes. And he *told* you that he was from Moscow?

JULIANNE: Yes.

PAUL: Well, that's... I mean, I... *(With an inkling of doubt...)* Is there... Well, there's another Moscow somewhere, right?

JULIANNE: Paul, when someone says they're from Moscow and has a Russian-seeming accent, where else can they be from?

PAUL: Then...why would he say that?

JULIANNE: *(With steadily growing concern)* I don't know, Paul. After all, we really don't know this man, do we? Other than that "Sam's cousin" recommended him.

PAUL: Jim's.

JULIANNE: *(Suddenly urgent...)* Whoever the hell it was. Jesus Christ, I'm calling the police...! *(She motions to phone on table...)*

PAUL: Well, wait a second, Julianne...

JULIANNE: Paul, this is it. I'm calling the Goddamn police.

PAUL: Don't call the police. There could be a logical explanation...

JULIANNE: *(As she dials and waits...)* I'm not gonna' wait to hear it, Paul, because, by then, we may very well be in his trunk.

PAUL: Julianne...

JULIANNE: This man is playing games with us, do you understand? Now are you going to protect your household or what?!

(VADISLAV, as before, seems to appear out of nowhere...)

VADISLAV: From...?

JULIANNE / PAUL: AHHHHHHHH!

(JULIANNE moves toward PAUL's side...)

PAUL: Julianne, it...it's fine, okay....?!

VADISLAV: I apologize. Protect from what?

JULIANNE: *(Hoping for a heroic action)* Paul?

PAUL: Um, Vad...Vadislav, um...we were just discussing how you...

(JULIANNE steps forward with phone clasped in hand...)

JULIANNE: *(Over "...how you...")* You have deceived us and you need to leave, alright?!! Now please go.

VADISLAV: *(A beat)* I apologize. It's true that I said I was simply going to relieve my bladder, but it seems to have become something else.

JULIANNE: What?!

VADISLAV: I had an adverse reaction to the tuna fish, I believe.

PAUL: Oh, God, I'm so sorry...

JULIANNE: Paul, don't apologize to him. Are you insane?!

PAUL: Well, I feel terrible.

JULIANNE: Paul...!

PAUL: I made it fresh today. How...?

JULIANNE: *Paul, will you wake up!* This man lied to us about something as simple as his regional origin, and that is a violation of consumer ethics.

VADISLAV: *(Taken aback)* I have made no such violation.

JULIANNE: Don't you question me in my house. Yes, you have!

VADISLAV: I have been completely honest with you in every respect. I have no reason to lie.

JULIANNE: *(Sharply and briskly)* You told me you were from Moscow.

VADISLAV: Yes.

JULIANNE: You told Paul that you were *not* from Russia.

VADISLAV: Yes.

JULIANNE: So what other "Moscow" are you referring to that's not in Russia, unless you were lying to at least one of us?

VADISLAV: I was referring to Idaho.

JULIANNE: *(Slight pause)* What?

VADISLAV: Moscow, Idaho.

PAUL: Idaho, the state?

VADISLAV: Of course. *(A beat)* You can google it, if you don't believe me.

JULIANNE: I asked where you were *from*. Where you were born and raised.

VADISLAV: That is where.

JULIANNE: *(A beat)* Moscow, Idaho.

VADISLAV: That's where I was born, yes. And later we moved to St. Petersburg.

PAUL: Russia?

VADISLAV: No. Florida.

JULIANNE: Then why do you have an accent?

VADISLAV: Well, my mother and father had the accent, so it just stuck to me, I suppose.

JULIANNE: And where were *they* from?

VADISLAV: From Stupino.

PAUL: Italy?

VADISLAV: No. Russia.

JULIANNE: *(Nearly trembling with both panic and rage...)* Jesus Christ, I'm fucking through with this.

(...as JULIANNE *marches towards the direction of the now barking Carrot, clasping phone...)*

VADISLAV: You asked where **I** was from, not where my *parents* were from.

JULIANNE: *(She dials...)* Jesus Christ...

VADISLAV: And Paul merely asked if I was from Russia and I told him honestly, no. I'm a proud American.

JULIANNE: He's playing with us. He's playing with me, and I don't have time...

(...the phone beeps, signaling that the battery is fading...)

JULIANNE: Shit! *(Aiming phone like a weapon...)* If you don't leave now, I will unleash Carrot on you, do you understand me?!!!

PAUL: Julianne, just wait a...

JULIANNE: PLEASE LEAVE MY HOME OR I WILL OPEN THAT SLIDING DOOR, DO YOU HEAR ME?!!!

VADISLAV: *(Pause, sincere and composed)* I am deeply sorry for any distress I may have caused either one of you,...but I can well assure you that I have not ever lied to either of you. I've shown you my license. My letter of recommendation. I've told you of mine and my parents' geographical origin. I even conveyed the unfortunate details of my bowel movement with more candor than is proper from a guest. And, as I have also indicated before, I will willingly leave if you wish, with no questions asked. But, if I do,...please know that I have been nothing but honest with you. *(Slight pause, with deeper resonance)* And,… if I may be permitted to say,…perhaps my presence has even allowed you both to be more honest with yourselves.

(A moment, as Carrot's barking subsides.)

JULIANNE: *(Somehow moved by this, yet unsettled.)* You… you were listening to us?

VADISLAV: *(A snicker)* How could I not? They could hear you in Russia.

(VADISLAV looks at both PAUL *and* JULIANNE *to see if he can generate a slight smile;* PAUL *reveals a tepid grin, while* JULIANNE *appears halted by the resonance of* VADISLAV'*s words.)*

(A moment)

VADISLAV: There is an old story, which I believe is true, about a married couple who always argued. Always. They fought like dogs, if you will. Every day it seemed they fought. The wife started something, the husband would react badly. The husband would start something, the wife would react badly. Back and forth, this went. Until one day, the husband and wife were in the midst of one of their now traditional fights, screaming at the top of their lungs over something tedious, when they came to a brief lull; a bare slice of silence between the thunder of their yells, wherein they heard the distant sobs of their children upstairs. *(A beat)* The couple vowed to each other at that moment that they would have to do things differently. They would have to relate to each other in a more humane way, and if they had to fight, they would channel their anger into something else. So if the wife was getting upset with the husband, she would instantly run to the kitchen and start cooking. She would take meat and slice it up viciously. Or she'd take potatoes and slice them into oblivion. And *he* would simply walk out

the door, and continue walking for blocks, sometimes
miles. Down dirt roads, through hills, up, down...
Now the children were still unsettled by this but at
least they could sleep. However, when their in-laws
would come to visit, they felt the need to intercede
and made a suggestion that the couple move to a
more soothing environment. More tropical, serene,
quiet. They agreed to it, for the sake of the children,
of course, but also for themselves, for things had not
always been as they had become between them. And
on rare occasion, they would even fleetingly remember
a time when they simply loved each other. *(A beat)*
And so within just a few weeks leading up to their
move, they would carry on as they were. They would
be nearing an argument, before the wife would run
to the kitchen; meat, potatoes, spinach... She would
some times make seven suppers in an evening based
on the level of her rage. And he would walk past the
town border, into the next town, into the next, without
so much as a heavy breath. So when they finally
arrived on this island, now with much less money, the
question became - could things change? Could they
simply exist together without this ubiquitous tension
that had previously plagued them. Could they fall in
love again? *(A beat)* Well, now they had no money,
very little food, and the husband struggled to find
work, which had never been the problem before. But
now, not only were these problems very real to them,
they were the *reason* for their anger at each other. Now
they were resentful of this move. They hated their in-
laws for this idea. The husband hated the wife for not
providing enough food, the wife hated the husband
for not providing enough money to *get* enough food.
So one day, almost paralyzed with rage, the wife ran
to the kitchen, retrieved the last remaining coconuts
from the pantry and chopped them violently, while
the husband walked out the door and continued on.

Only, because they were on an island, he only had a
few acres of sand before reaching the ocean. His anger
and resentment were so lethal, that all he could do was
continue on, walking onto the ocean floor for nearly
a mile...before eventually being devoured by sharks.
(A beat) And the wife... Well, she would soon run out
of food to prepare,...so she killed her children...and
cooked *them. (A beat)* She would remain on the island,
alone,...for the rest of her life.

(A still moment, as JULIANNE *and* PAUL *are stunned.)*

JULIANNE: *(Shaken)* So...what is...what is the point of
this story?

VADISLAV: *(A half-joke)* Well, the point is that marriage
is very difficult. *(Pause, profoundly)* The point is...that,
perhaps, the problem is not that Carrot hates your
husband or your daughter. It's that Carrot identifies
with *you,*...because *you* hate them.

(A stunned, considerable silence)

JULIANNE: I...I...I... How...? That's unbe... How
can...? How can...how can you say such a...?

PAUL: *(With suspicion...)* Why did you get Carrot,
Julianne?

JULIANNE: *(A beat, taken aback)* What do you...? You...
you know why.

PAUL: Because Brittany said she wanted a dog?

JULIANNE: Yes.

PAUL: I never heard her say that. When I asked her,...
she said she may have mentioned it once, but it wasn't
logical to her since we had Wolfgang. She didn't really
want a dog, because I would've known it.

JULIANNE: She wanted a dog. She said that.

PAUL: When?

JULIANNE: At…at more than one point, she said it…

PAUL: This dog wasn't for her. It was never for her.

JULIANNE: I could give my daughter a gift, Paul. You're not the only one who has that privilege.

PAUL: You didn't get it for her. She didn't want the damn dog. You got it for yourself, and you didn't give a shit if she already had Wolfgang. You didn't care because you hated the cat, you hate her and you hate me…!

JULIANNE: *(Between rage and immense sadness)* GOD DAMN YOU, THERE IS NO HATRED IN MY HOME!!! *(A still moment)* You have the audacity… My God, you'll never be able to fathom what's… You've never known what it's like to be part of a family and feel alone, let alone feel it *twice.* You had everything since the womb, Paul, and yet all you've become is resentful of me, and all I did is come from *nothing* and make something of myself. I was adopted by cretinous parents in a disgusting home, and look at what I've accomplished, and yet all I am in this house is someone who's capable of hating her own family?! A daughter I helped to raise, a husband I used to…to… Only to be… only to be excluded?! *(A beat) You have not a clue, Paul. (A considerable pause. She becomes choked up in this rare, vulnerable moment, though she gathers somewhat, before speaking to no one in particular, at first.)* I was on my way home one day…after meeting with a client. It was my highest paying job to that point and, yet,…I felt so empty. Maybe because…I knew what I was coming home to. So,…on my way home, I happened to drive past an animal shelter, which I'd been by before. On this day, though, I guess, I felt…like I was returning to my roots or something. Like I had to go back to save myself. I saw all these poor eager dogs. Jumping up, barking, crying out… My God, what they wouldn't

give for someone to just…to…you know, just take
them home. I'd never even had a dog, but… *(Slight
pause)* And then…I saw Carrot. Alone in that cage,
with…with his poor ear. So solemn, but so beautiful.
It was…unacceptable to me that he was there, on
that yellowed newspaper… *(As if transported to the
moment…)* And there was no doubt that he belonged
with me. It was…it was as if we were soul mates. God,
he saved me as much as I saved him. I needed him to…
protect, and to have a sense of protection myself. My
whole life, I've always felt that I had to protect myself.
Guard myself. I had no one else. I didn't as a child,…
and I don't anymore as a wife, but…now I have Carrot.
(To PAUL, *near tears…)* That's not hatred. *(A beat)*
That's…that's the only love I know anymore.

(A still moment, with JULIANNE *consumed by her own
revelation, …while* PAUL *and* VADISLAV *observe.)*

VADISLAV: Which brings me to my next question; are
you having intimate relations with Carrot?

*(*JULIANNE *looks at* VADISLAV, *barely able to fathom…)*

JULIANNE: *(Pause)* What…what the hell did you just ask
me?

VADISLAV: A question.

JULIANNE: Am I…am I having sexual relations with my
dog?

VADISLAV: Again, it is merely a question.

JULIANNE: It is not "merely" anything, you fucking
asshole! How can you ask such a thing?

VADISLAV: It's not the most unusual thing in my line of
work…

JULIANNE: Fuck you!

VADISLAV: So the answer is "no".

JULIANNE: Yes, the Goddamn answer is…! How can…? After opening myself up like I just did, and you ask such a… *(A beat, both with anger and a sense of betrayal)* I want you outa' my house right now!

(A beat, while VADISLAV *retrieves bag…)*

PAUL: Actually, I've…sort of considered it myself.

*(*VADISLAV *stops.)*

JULIANNE: *(A beat)* You've what?

PAUL: *(Not proud of this…)* Well, not the…not the actual *sex* part…maybe…but…I…I dunno, I guess I've felt that there was something you both found in each other that no one could interfere with.

JULIANNE: Are you out of your fucking mind?!

PAUL: I'm just saying the thought has crossed…

JULIANNE: It's crossed the mind that you're out of?! It's…it's crossed your mind, and yet it's been so easy for you to let a *dog* intercede in your relationship with your wife?

PAUL: I haven't let the dog…

JULIANNE: *(Over "the dog…")* Oh, no, you haven't **let** it, right? God forbid you be manipulated by idiot co-workers you don't even like, a stranger from Moscow fucking Idaho… So how on earth can a German Shepard manipulate you, right?

PAUL: I'm not saying that…

JULIANNE: *(Over "…not saying that…")* This is the Goddamn limit.

PAUL: I didn't accuse…

JULIANNE: You say this isn't about blame?! That's *exactly* what this is; to you and to you. You *want* it to be my fault. *I'm* the problem here, despite all I've ever done for you; put you on my back in New York when

you couldn't so much as get out of bed. Forced myself
into your arms just to get a sign of life from you…
If I didn't get pregnant with Brittany, you probably
would've killed yourself. But *I'm* to blame! *Carrot* is to
blame because of…because of some sort of depraved
lust we share, while you just sit idly by…?!

PAUL: How could I bring something like this up?!

JULIANNE: *Exactly, Paul! How could you?! Unless you're
just trying to deflect your own heinous behavior.*

PAUL: What the hell are you…?

JULIANNE: *(Over "…are you…?")* You are not my
husband…and you sure as hell are not any sort of
parental figure to our daughter…

PAUL: Do not bring Brittany into this…

JULIANNE: *You* brought her into this, Paul…

PAUL: DO NOT BRING BRITTANY INTO THIS, DO
YOU HEAR ME?!!! That…that kid's gotten everything
from me. EVERYTHING! I couldn't be more
supportive of her, while you come down on her like
a…like a bitchy avalanche. She can't breathe around
you. No one can. Is it any wonder that she doesn't
approach you. That I don't? She was already afraid
of you, then you got Carrot and she can barely stand
to be in the house now. So…you know, I may not be
your husband as of this moment, and you may not be
my wife, but if you think I'm not a father to Brittany,
you're wrong, because regardless of your relationship
with that dog, you have long since driven her way. If
she doesn't have me, she's an orphan, do you hear me?
She has nothing but her oboe, *which she fucking hates
anyway!*

(JULIANNE *is frozen by this for a moment…*)

JULIANNE: I want a divorce.

PAUL: No more than I do, believe me.

JULIANNE: And don't think for a second that I'm letting you walk away with Brittany.

PAUL: I'm her father.

JULIANNE: I'm her mother.

PAUL: But you don't even have time to be. You get this show, what, you're gonna' have maids raise her? What kind of childhood is that?!

JULIANNE: *Better that than…!*

(A moment, as JULIANNE *halts, but looks resentfully at* PAUL.*)*

VADISLAV: Then…what?

JULIANNE: *(Slight pause, with a pained grin)* Are you sure you want me to say, Paul? Vadislav may not want to stay for dessert.

PAUL: *(Seemingly clueless…)* What…what are you…? I don't know what you're… *(A beat)* What are you saying now?

(A moment, as JULIANNE *can barely speak this. Her humiliation outsizing her bitterness now…)*

JULIANNE: I noticed… *(Slight pause)*   Paul,…I noticed.

PAUL: Noticed…? What…? *(To* VADISLAV, *then* JULIANNE*)* I don't know what the hell you're talking about?

JULIANNE: *(Slight pause, becoming choked up)* About a year ago. You used to look at *me* like that.

(A moment)

PAUL: What…? Julianne, I really hope you're not saying…that you're even fathoming where I think you're…

JULIANNE: You think she's changed. She has. And I think I may know why.

(A moment, as PAUL *can only turn to* VADISLAV, *then to* JULIANNE...)

PAUL: This is unbe...I can't believe what...what you're suggesting.

JULIANNE: I'm asking.

PAUL: What the hell are you asking?

VADISLAV: I can translate, if you wish.

PAUL: *(Gently escorting him to the door...)* Alright, we're done here. Vadislav, I'm sorry but I guess you can see that we'll be divorcing so we won't be needing your services after all...

JULIANNE: He can stay.

PAUL: We don't need him anymore.

JULIANNE: *You* don't need him.

PAUL: It's very clear that we won't be in this house much longer, so...

JULIANNE: *You* won't.

PAUL: *We* won't!

JULIANNE: Brittany will be here.

PAUL: No, she won't, Julianne.

JULIANNE: Yes, she will. You're not taking her from me.

PAUL: She's my daughter.

JULIANNE: She's my daughter as well!

PAUL: If I leave her here, that dog will kill her!!!

VADISLAV: You believe this.

PAUL: Yes, I believe...! For Godsakes, can't you see what this woman is like?! She'll stoop to nothing to make me look like...like I'm not even human. I mean,

Jesus Christ, look what she came from? Her mother
sold her horn for booze, so she's forced an oboe down
her daughter's throat. Doesn't that tell you? She's
become what she says she never wanted to be. She
doesn't know how to convey warmth, love, support,
except to the fucking dog. If it doesn't kill Brittany
first, then she'll be driven to suicide by the time she
graduates. She's not safe here by herself.

VADISLAV: And she's safe with you.

PAUL: Yes, she's safe with me! I'm her father.

VADISLAV: And you think she's safer with you than
with your wife and Carrot?

PAUL: Of course I do! What, you think she's better off
having a German Shepard for a father figure?

JULIANNE: You go to hell!

VADISLAV: No worse than a father who acts like a
husband.

PAUL: *(Slight pause, enraged!)* Get the hell out of my
house.

JULIANNE: Stay!

PAUL: GET OUT!

VADISLAV: Shall we flip a coin?

(PAUL *charges at* VADISLAV…)

PAUL: I WANT YOU OUT OF THIS GODDAMN…!!!

(In stride, PAUL *swings at* VADISLAV *who, in turn, catches*
PAUL's *arm with a single hand. He holds it in place for a
moment, before slowly driving* PAUL *back to couch, as if in
slow motion. He sits him down, as if* PAUL *has lost control
of his own body.)*

(JULIANNE *observes, speechless.)*

VADISLAV: You have been gracious hosts up to this
point. There is no need for physical confrontation.

Be thankful I have considered both of your opinions equally throughout this day.

PAUL: *(Slight pause, stunned himself)* Al…alright. I'm sorry…

VADISLAV: Apology accepted. *(A beat, as he looks at* JULIANNE.*)* Julianne, please sit across from your husband.

JULIANNE: *(A beat, looks at* PAUL, *then* VADISLAV…*)* But…why? This really isn't necess….

PAUL: *(Attempts to rise…)* I said I was sorry for…for…*I can't get up!*

VADISLAV: It's a canine restraint tactic. A temporary disability. It'll wear off shortly, I promise.

PAUL: What are you going to do?

VADISLAV: What I have been hired to do. *(To* JULIANNE*)* Now please.

*(*JULIANNE *takes a cautious moment, before nervously doing so.* VADISLAV *approaches* JULIANNE *and* PAUL. *A beat)*

VADISLAV: Scootch a bit so that you are directly facing each other.

JULIANNE / PAUL: Oh, my God… / *Don't hurt her, please!*

VADISLAV: *(Slight pause)* Hurt her…?

PAUL: I said I was sorry for coming at you, okay? Don't do this!

VADISLAV: This is not a punishment. That is not my role here. Now, please,…scootch.

(A moment, before JULIANNE *slides over a bit so that she and* PAUL *are directly facing each other.* VADISLAV *then moves behind* PAUL.*)*

VADISLAV: A child never wins in a situation such as this. Regardless of what you both may have done,

directly or indirectly, chances are that she has long
since lost. Her self-esteem. Her self-worth. Her feeling
of safety within her own home. *(To* PAUL*)* Perhaps her
virginity.

PAUL: *(Indignantly)* I have not laid a hand on her in any
unsavory way.

VADISLAV: No?

PAUL: *Absolutely not!*

VADISLAV: *(To* JULIANNE*)* Do you believe this?

PAUL: Why are you doing this?

VADISLAV: I haven't done anything. You've done this to
yourself.

PAUL: I haven't done anything except be husband to
my wife and a father to my daughter.

VADISLAV: Is that true?

PAUL: YES, IT'S TRUE!

VADISLAV: I'm asking your wife.

PAUL: You don't need to ask her. She hasn't seen
anything. She's making something up so that she looks
responsible.

VADISLAV: There is no more responsibility on her end if
she suspected something and failed to react.

JULIANNE: *(To* PAUL, *torn yet sadly consumed by the
notion.)* I didn't want to admit to the possibility.

PAUL: *(To* JULIANNE*)* Nothing happened, do you
understand?!

VADISLAV: Nothing.

PAUL: NOTHING!!!

*(Carrot barks, as he will throughout the next sequence, as
VADISLAV suddenly lowers himself closer to PAUL, who
struggles, but is unable, to rise...)*

VADISLAV: If I were judge and jury and you had to tell me the truth so help you God, what would you say?

PAUL: I would say what I'm saying...

VADISLAV: What would you say?!

PAUL / JULIANNE: Why are you...? / Oh, God, please...

VADISLAV: Honesty is the only policy!

PAUL / JULIANNE: I'm telling you...! / No, don't ask him.

VADISLAV: What would you say?!

PAUL: I'm telling you...!

VADISLAV: WHAT WOULD YOU SAY?!

PAUL: *(Painfully, as if an exorcism...)* IT WAS ONLY A LOOK!!!

(A moment,...before VADISLAV *takes a step back. The barking has ceased.)*

(A beat)

VADISLAV: A look.

(A still moment. The following is delivered very gradually, with an incremental build...)

PAUL: *(Deeply...)* One. That was it. I never did anything. I never ever, *ever* would. *I'm her father, Julianne. (Pause, with immense pain...)* I'd just...I'd been sad. *(A beat)* Wolfgang had recently...*vanished*,...and you'n I had just had an argument about...something. I don't remember what,...but you won, of course.,... and I was... feeling very... I was in...despair. About a lot of things. And...then Brittany came home, and...I had had a few glasses of wine at that point, and...I...I looked at her differently, and that's...that's what you saw. I remember. *(A beat, near tears...)* Because I wanted you to. *(Pause, as his movement slowly and unconsciously returns...)* When...when we drove down

from New York, and you were pregnant, God, I…I
remember feeling…like things were going to be…
Maybe I wasn't going to be a chef like I dreamed, but
I… We were happy. Y'know? It was… *(Slight pause,
with weakened nostalgia.)* And then when Brittany was
born,…I remember feeling as if the three of *us* were on
an island…and we were all that we had. And I liked
feeling how we were…we were creating ourselves
anew, you and I, and we were raising Brittany as if
the possibilities for her were…endless. *(A beat)* But…
things changed,…and…I'm to blame for that as
much as you. I'll admit that…I'd lost confidence in…
in furthering myself,…but I *was* still a working and
supportive husband and father. I did have pride in
that, Julianne,…and yet you…you made me feel like
I had to keep pace with your success. It got to a point
where I…I couldn't talk to you without feeling… I
mean, Jesus, I got enough of that from my father,
and now… And I know, you came from nothing, and
wanted everything. And it got to where you wanted
everybody to be on your tenacious level. But that's just
not who we are. It's not who I am. I don't even know
who the hell that is anymore. *(A beat)* And Brittany
started to feel the same way, and so…for a time there,
she was…we listened to each other…a little more than
we used to. Always a father and daughter, but …we
were just…there for each other more. And I know you
resented that. My God, you…you had us feeling as if
we were conspiring against you, to the point where
she pulled away from *both* of us…. I mean, Jesus
Christ, I just wanted us to be a loving family, and now
I couldn't even speak to my daughter without… *(A
beat, with increasingly pained frustration)* And, for the
last several years, when I tried to approach you…
like a husband,…you were not approachable. You
haven't been. And…you aren't now, Julianne. *(Slight
pause)* And once you got Carrot, the best of you was…

with him. *(Pause, internally at first)* So...in a moment of...feeling very...low,...while she watched T V, I...I looked at her... like I used to look at *you*. But she never saw me. I didn't want her to. *(A beat, eventually to* JULIANNE.*)* I only wanted *you* to...because...I wanted to hurt you,...and I am ashamed of that, Julianne. But that was it. *(A beat, emotionally emphatic)* She's my daughter. *(Slight pause, near tears)* I know you don't hate her. And I don't think you hate me. And I don't hate you. Jesus, I...I used to love you. *(Slight pause)* But...we've failed each other, Julianne.

*(*VADISLAV *observes both* JULIANNE *and* PAUL.*)*

(A still moment)

JULIANNE: *(With deep regret)* You're right. *(Slight pause)* We have.

*(*PAUL *now an open wound of exposed pain, and* JULIANNE *visibly distraught, more by the content of his words than anything else. They are almost oblivious to* VADISLAV.*)*

VADISLAV: I believe you. I believe you both. *(Slight pause)* I do not believe that there is evil in either of you. I've simply concluded that you are two people who have...lost the ability to love each other. And a marriage without love is cancerous, particularly to the child. *(Pause)* I'm going to ask one last thing. *(A beat)* Do you remember the moment when you realized you were in love with each other?

(A moment, as JULIANNE *and* PAUL *face each other, unable to fathom anything beyond this day, these moments...)*

JULIANNE: *(Softly, with deep regret)* No.

PAUL: *(A beat, the same)* No.

VADISLAV: *(Pause, digesting this with disappointment)* I see. *(After a moment of stillness, with gentle efficiency...)* That said,...I will now see Carrot.

(This breaks PAUL *and* JULIANNE *out of their states somewhat, disoriented...)*

JULIANNE: You...you what?

VADISLAV: I will see Carrot.

PAUL: But...so much has... I mean, it... Brittany's not even...

VADISLAV: I know what I need to know. Excuse me.

*(*VADISLAV *exits off, while* PAUL *and* JULIANNE *look at each other, drained yet perplexed. She rises urgently, as does he, but awkwardly remain in living room.)*

(There has been some distant growling from Carrot, which gets louder and more violent once we hear the sliding doors open. Just as it appears that the hideous growls will lead to an outright attack,...there is a sudden silence.)

*(*JULIANNE *and* PAUL *look off, as she moves toward patio,... before we hear a happy bark, as if a sudden metamorphosis of Carrot. They are still uncertain as to what is happening, coupled with their emotional fatigue.)*

(We hear the sliding door close, before VADISLAV *re-enters. The entire procedure has taken no more than thirty seconds.)*

VADISLAV: *(With his usual removed efficiency)* It is done. *(He comes into living area...)*

JULIANNE: I...what...?

PAUL: You're kidding. You...you...

VADISLAV: It is done. He is fine. He understands.

JULIANNE / PAUL: He...he understands...? / He what...he...?

VADISLAV: Yes. *(A beat, gently yet profoundly)* Now *you* must. Whatever becomes of the two of you,...you must understand; you are responsible. For Carrot. For Brittany.—For it all. *(A beat)* It is now up to you.

(A still moment, his words having halted JULIANNE *and* PAUL.*)*

(A car pulls up.)

PAUL: That…that's…that's Brittany. Would you…like to…?

VADISLAV: I will say hello. Nothing more. I am done. *(He goes to door, turns to them…)* Be well. *(He exits, closes door.)*

(A moment…before JULIANNE *goes to couch, slowly. She is depleted, overwhelmed…*PAUL *gazes at door.)*

*(*JULIANNE *sits, gazing out…and begins to sob, slowly and, eventually, convulsively.)*

(Similar to earlier, PAUL *notices* JULIANNE, *looks at her for a moment while his own emotion builds…)*

*(*PAUL *slowly approaches, sits beside* JULIANNE…*and aggressively wraps his arms around her, as he too begins to sob. They hold each other, if not with a hope then with a primal desperation.)*

(The front door soon opens, which they observe, …still in their embrace.)

(Lights out)

END OF PLAY

AUTHOR'S NOTES

It should be clear that the play is intended to move briskly. Of course, this is aside from the indicated beats, moments and pauses, which should be adhered to.

On the characters— It may appear more clear as to what the intentions are of Paul than that of Julianne, on the surface. Paul wants to resolve the issue with Carrot and thus seemingly create greater stability in the house, which is controlled more by Julianne. Julianne's desires are more suppressed and ambiguous. In the playing of her, it should be established that she has relinquished control of the Carrot issue to Paul, who obviously feels greater urgency, though she has done so begrudgingly as, we later find out, she has the better relationship with Carrot. One can also say that she has done it *subconsciously*, with a desire for PAUL to prove himself in some way to her, even though she is probably expectant of an adverse result.

It should be also known that Julianne *does* want this to work, at the beginning. However, she does not deem this a complex situation and, therefore, it is the complexities that develop which become frustrating for her. The fact that Vadislav makes some unusual demands and that Paul doesn't necessarily have all the information before him and ultimately appears to be losing control of the situation is what makes her impatient, suspicious, protective, ill-at-ease, and

ultimately hostile. However, from the beginning
she should do her best to keep a "best face" on, as
Paul does. Paul, obviously, does this better. But, in
truth, nothing she is asking of Paul or Vadislav is
unreasonable through much of the first act. She is a
busy woman and, in truth, her work and Carrot are the
best things in her life which, as we learn, are ultimately
not enough and are filling large voids within her.

What ultimately gives the play its drive is as much
Paul's convictions to "remedy" the familial situation
as it is Julianne's to do so on *her* terms. Of course, this
dovetails into the deeper revelations that they are
needing to convey more than either is consciously
aware of; Julianne living in response to overcoming
her past which has been magnified by the resentment
of the present, regardless of what she has adversely
contributed to it, which is also true of Paul, in that
what he has become (especially regarding his career)
stands in stark contrast to what he once aspired.

Vadislav is very much in keeping with his character
description. He is obviously a source of intrigue and
humor, which will not require any great exaggeration,
and his stern façade can precede the more nuanced
aspects of his enigmatic personality. He never imposes
his will to stay, and remains through the insistence of
either Paul or Julianne.

*It is also important to note that, in keeping with
Vadislav's enigmatic nature, he is ultimately what Paul
and/or Julianne empower him to be. The revelation
of Paul's "look" regarding Brittany is not intended
to be a bombshell intended to confound. Though it is
addressed out of Julianne's bitterness and resentment
of Paul, it is delivered with immense pain and
humiliation, and Paul's ultimate admittance of this
action should be equally so; his reasoning should be

an honest, deeply personal expression that ultimately supersedes Vadislav's intimidation.